JOHN WESLEY

JOHN WESLEY
A PREACHING LIFE

MICHAEL PASQUARELLO III

Abingdon Press
Nashville

JOHN WESLEY
A PREACHING LIFE

Copyright © 2010 by Abingdon Press

All rights reserved.

This book is printed on acid-free paper.

Library of Congress Cataloging-in-Publication Data

Pasquarello, Michael.
  John Wesley : a preaching life / Michael Pasquarello III.
    p. cm.
  ISBN 978-0-687-65756-8 (binding: book--pbk. : alk. paper)
  1. Wesley, John, 1703-1791. I. Title.
  BX8495.W5P37 2010
  252'.07--dc22

                     2009054422

All scripture quotations are taken from the New Revised Standard Version of the Bible, copyright 1989, Division of Christian Education of the National Council of the Churches of Christ in the United States of America. Used by permission. All rights reserved.

Chapter 2 contains revised material originally published in Michael Pasquarello III, *Sacred Rhetoric: Preaching as Theological and Pastoral Practice of the Church* © 2005 Wm B. Eerdmans Publishing Company, Grand Rapids, Michigan. Reprinted by permission of the publisher, all rights reserved.

Selections from "The End of Wesleyan Theology" by William Abraham are taken from the *Wesleyan Theological Journal*, 40:1 (Spring 2005): 7-25.

10 11 12 13 14 15 16 17 18 19—10 9 8 7 6 5 4 3 2 1

MANUFACTURED IN THE UNITED STATES OF AMERICA

CONTENTS

PREFACE

I want to express my deep gratitude to Abingdon Press for the opportunity to work on this project. I am also indebted to many scholars in the field of Wesleyan studies who have helped me understand more clearly the significance of Wesley's thought, life, and ministry. I could not have attempted this book without their work. However, my primary intention in writing is to converse with students, preachers, and homileticians who identify themselves as members of the various Wesleyan families. It is also my hope that students, pastors, and teachers of preachers from other Christian traditions will find in John Wesley a salutary witness to the evangelical and catholic spirit of the gospel we have been called to believe, live, and proclaim for the praise of God's glory.

Some thirty years ago, when I was received into the membership of The United Methodist Church, I knew nothing of John Wesley's deep roots in the Christian tradition. Since then, it has been my great joy to discover that the people called "Methodists" are the descendants of a rich heritage of doctrine, liturgy, and discipline that may yet serve as a means of returning us to know and love the Triune God who is our final good and happiness. I would not have come to appreciate this heritage without the guidance of teachers at Duke Divinity School who encouraged me, as a novice theological student, to listen and learn from the wisdom of the Christian tradition: Dr. David Steinmetz, Dr. Robert E. Cushman, Dr. McMurray Richey, Dr. Charles K. Robinson, Dr. Stuart Henry, Dr. John Westerhoff. In recent years, I have benefited from many conversations with colleagues and students at Asbury Theological Seminary around the subject of Wesley and the Christian past. Finally, this book is dedicated to the men and women who continue to proclaim the gospel in the tradition of Methodist preachers and preaching, or the "preaching life."

A HOMILETIC THEOLOGIAN

During almost three decades of pastoral ministry I have heard John Wesley invoked as an authority for preaching to produce results described as "evangelism" and "social justice." What I noticed, however, in the desire to emulate Wesley's presumably effective methods and the enthusiasm for replicating his obviously impressive results—as an evangelist and as an agent of social change—was a pervasive tendency to forget or even dispense with the convictions, dispositions, and habits that oriented his life and ministry to the knowledge and love of God. In most instances, very little of substance was said about the doctrinal clarity and spiritual wisdom of his sermons, his vision of the church as a people called to a life of holiness and happiness, or his deep roots in the doctrinal, liturgical, and pastoral heritage of the Church of England and the larger Christian tradition.

I was left with the impression that Wesley's significance is often reduced to that of a distant historical source for underwriting contemporary expressions of theological revisionism, religious experience, pragmatic ministry, and social ethics for which God is either altogether dispensable or instrumentally useful for the goals we have chosen. William Abraham describes the consequences of doctrinal erosion by which the ontological moorings of Wesleyan doctrine are separated from the truth and reality of God, creating a kind of "boring theological archeology."

> Negatively, this is expressed in terms of impatience with the past and in terms of critical analyses which have no sympathy with the deep inner spirit of the tradition. Positively it is expressed in terms of a quest for action and relevance which tends to focus on this or that aspect of the tradition without taking full measure of its content. They become treated with increasing suspicion until one reaches the point where they are either forgotten or despised.[1]

After an extended time of study in the Christian tradition, especially the history of preaching and its preachers, I began to reread Wesley in conversation with the Christian past. Much to my surprise, I recognized in his work the kind of theological orientation and practical wisdom I had come to see in the work of preaching theologians from earlier periods in the church's life.

During this time I also happened upon an essay by Albert Outler that challenged me to make sense of Wesley's life and ministry, as well as my own, in light of the larger ecclesial and theological tradition we share.

> Wesley has been invoked oftener than he has been read and usually has been read with a low-church, anti-intellectual bias that celebrates his warm heart and worn saddlebags, unconcerned with his theology. But this very pathos could rescue the study of Wesley from the genetic fallacy that haunts most denominational histories. It is more important, I have come to believe, to study Wesley's theology in the light of his antecedents than his successors.[2]

This book is a modest attempt in this direction. My hope is that we might hear Wesley in fresh ways that will allow him to be more than instrumentally useful for our goals and agendas. My aim, then, has been to read Wesley as a faithful exemplar, teacher, and mentor; a homiletic theologian whose work may help us to rediscover for our ourselves the joy of his ministry: that the truth is God matters in every aspect of our preaching. Rather than seeing Wesley as a historical source with limited usefulness for today, I assume his work is instructive, challenging, and even disturbing for our time. In other words, I assume Wesley wants to convert us; to make us holy as God is holy. For this reason, I have approached Wesley as a teacher and exemplar of particular habits of the heart and mind that are necessary for becoming faithful readers and speakers of Scripture as the Word of God. In other words, becoming a certain kind of person, called by God and the church for the ministry of the Word, is fundamentally a matter of theological judgment, spiritual maturity, and clarity of moral vision.

This book examines Wesley's homiletic wisdom in light of select conversations with the Christian past that help to illumine his convictions, habits, and words as an exemplar of the preaching life. At the same time, it presumes to provide neither a detailed historical study of his life and thought nor a comprehensive analysis of his sermons.[3] Rather, my aim is more modest and specific. My hope is that attending to Wesley as a homiletic theologian may yet guide us to see that the truth of God matters in every aspect of preaching.[4]

Wesley's work demonstrates a steadfast commitment to reading, thinking, and speaking theologically, that is, with the conviction that, as a means of grace, the use of Scripture in the life of the church mediates the truth and goodness of Christ through the work of the Holy Spirit. Learning to preach like Wesley does not mean devising strategies for replicating his accomplishments and results; rather, learning to preach like Wesley means discerning the character of his practical wisdom to become more thoughtful speakers of the truth in love with God and our neighbors—especially those neighbors whom we address as "listeners." And while we do not possess a single book or treatise on preaching from Wesley, much of his work, especially the written sermons, can be read as a kind of *summa homiletica*—a summary of homiletic theology—for instructing preachers in the language and "grammar" of living faith and holy living.[5] Thus, as a preacher and teacher of preachers, Wesley's work encourages us to be more faithful ministers of the gospel in assisting the Spirit's work of evangelizing and transforming listeners to become participants in the way, truth, and life of Jesus Christ.[6]

Or to put this differently, Wesley's sermons articulate a trinitarian discourse in intimate relation to the life of a preacher and those who listen. Divine revelation was the constant and rhetoric the variable in his preaching, so that knowing and loving the Triune God was of greater importance than choosing the right homiletic method, technique, or skill. In other words, no amount of homiletic strategy, moves, eloquence, illustrations, techniques, and experimental forms of effective communication are sufficient substitutes for the presence and work of the Holy Spirit renewing both speakers and listeners in the image of God made known in Christ. For Wesley, the being and life of the church is a gift of the Triune God whose truth and goodness are received through prayer, the liturgy, preaching, the sacraments, catechesis, and a life of discipleship ordered by the wisdom of holiness.

Although Wesley is viewed as one the most effective preachers in Christian history, he did not view the effects of preaching as a result of doing what works by reducing the work of God to method and skill. Rather the results of ministry were seen as the effect of being drawn to faith in God's self-communicative activity by the agency of the Spirit who transforms us to think, act, and speak with the mind of Christ. As a result, Wesley's preaching summoned listeners to a life of repentance and wholehearted devotion to God's kingdom in the life, death, and resurrection of Jesus who reigns with the Father by the power of the Holy Spirit.[7] For Wesley, this occurs by

> the power of God attending his Word he brings these sinners to repentance: an entire inward as well as outward change, from all evil to all good. And this is in a sound sense to "cast out devils," out of the souls wherein they had hitherto dwelt. The strong one can no longer keep his house. A stronger than he has come upon him, and hath cast him out, and taken possession for himself, and made it an habitation of God through his Spirit. Here than the energy of Satan end, and the Son of God "destroys the works of the devil." The understanding of the sinner is now enlightened, and is heartly sweetly drawn to God. His desires are refined, his affections purified; and being filled with the Holy Ghost he grows in grace till he is not only holy in heart, but in all manner of conversation.[8]

Such convictions are grounded in the church's trinitarian confession of faith and make Wesley, as a "preaching theologian," interesting and challenging for our time. As much contemporary homiletic practice demonstrates, the liberation of preaching from substantive engagement with the truth of doctrine for nothing but freedom itself has effectively separated the intellect from the will, creating forms of religion that make God dispensable other than for utilitarian purposes. In other words, the flight from reason illumined by grace through faith, to empirically derived means of making Christianity relevant and useful for today, can do nothing other than produce preaching deficient in theological judgment, spiritual wisdom, and pastoral discernment.

A practical consequence of such "de-regulated" communication—devoid of doctrinal wisdom—is more talking points than theological convictions and more talking heads than faithful witnesses to the gospel. Proclaiming the truth of God's reign in Jesus Christ is not the same as trusting the logic of a religious market and its economy to determine the church's identity and mission.[9] As one Wesleyan theologian writes,

Authentic Christianity, in the Wesleyan understanding, is a Christianity of radical transformation. It has nothing to do with straightening out one's life, cleaning up damaging addictions, or taking the moral high ground. These will likely be some of the consequences of that transformation, but they are not the source of it. Christ alone is that source. When people come to him in repentance and faith they enter a new relationship with God and a new life in Christ.[10]

On the other hand, Wesley's homiletic discourse was thoroughly trinitarian in bearing witness to the cosmic scope of the new creation inaugurated by Christ in the power of the Spirit; the truth that the church receives, celebrates, embodies, and proclaims to the world through the illumination and empowerment of the Spirit.

> [God] is already renewing the face of the earth. And we have strong reason to hope that the work he hath begun, he will carry on unto the day of the Lord Jesus; that he will never intermit this blessed work of his Spirit, until he has fulfilled all his promises; until he hath put a period to sin, and misery, and infirmity, and death; and re-established universal holiness and happiness, and caused all the inhabitants of the earth to sing together, "Hallelujah, the Lord God omnipotent reigneth!"[11]

Wesley resisted the displacement of God by the modern orthodoxy of "relevance" that has liberated preaching from its primary concern for truth to become an independent source of religious experience and social ethics. Charles Taylor describes this as self-sufficient or "external" humanism that is unwilling to accept any goals beyond its own flourishing or any allegiances beyond itself; a vision which effectively makes God useless and irrelevant.[12] However, as Stephen Long observes, modern humanisms of the "subject-centered self" may now be as antiquated as Wesley's theology, so that belief in humanity, culture, technology, self-help, and social progress will require more of a sacrifice of the intellect than faith in the Triune God. He writes of Wesley's theology:

> Once the focus of Wesley's theology becomes relevant "for today" in a North American context, it is easy to see how his work can be retrospectively read as a protopragmatism. However, this may have more to do with modern theologians' fetishization of the modern than with Wesley, for it takes an imaginative act to

read Wesley in terms of this pragmatist narrative where the "practical" Wesley, whose theology responds to "needs" replaces the dogmatic Wesley committed to metaphysical principles of truth and creedal Christianity.[13]

Of all the genres in the Wesley corpus, the written sermons focus and expound a homiletic theology that springs from and leads to the truth and goodness of the gospel he believed, lived, and proclaimed. Wesley describes this as the happiness of the Christian religion, a life that consists of knowing and loving God; the way of holiness that bears fruit in good works and words and witnesses the truth of God in human life. The preface to the 1746 edition of *Sermons on Several Occasions* describes Wesley's desire to know and communicate the way of holiness and happiness in God.

> I want to know one thing, the way to heaven—how to land safe on that happy shore. God himself has condescended to teach the way: for this very end he came from heaven. He hath written it down in a book. O give me that book! Give me the Book of God! . . . I have accordingly set down in the following sermons what I find in the Bible concerning the way to heaven, with a view to distinguish this way of God from all those which are the inventions of men. I have endeavoured to describe the true, the scriptural, experimental religion, so as to omit nothing which is a real part thereof, and to add nothing thereto which is not.[14]

Springing from the knowledge and love of God, such holy and happy preaching entails the transformation of the intellect, affections, and will through the work of Christ and the Holy Spirit that restores us to the divine image, the most definitive form of human receptivity to the Word. Through prayerful attentiveness to the divine realities revealed in Scripture we receive new habits of the heart and mind that enable us to think, speak, and live according to the wisdom and virtue of Christ.[15] "Prayer is our entrance into the grammar of revelation, the grammar of the word of God."[16] By listening to God, moreover, we are formed into a life of spiritual and moral excellence through the Spirit's gifts, virtues, and fruit, learning to love and advancing in hope, bearing witness to "a beauty, a love, a holiness."[17] Wesley writes of knowing God,

> We may learn hence, . . . that this happy knowledge of the true God is only another name for religion; I mean Christian religion, which indeed is the only

one that deserves the name. Religion, as to the nature or essence of it, does not lie in this or that set of notions, vulgarily called 'faith'; nor in a round of duties, however carefully 'reformed' from error and superstition. It does not consist in any number of outward actions. No; it properly and directly consists in the knowledge and love of God, as manifested in the Son of his love, through the eternal Spirit. And this naturally leads to every heavenly temper, and to every good word and work.[18]

The significance of witness has been emphasized by Robert Wilken who observes that authority has to do with the truthful quality, trustworthiness, and testimony of a person's life; that trusting in authority is a necessary part of the knowledge received by faith. Wilken comments:

This is not primarily a matter of gaining information, but involves habits, attitudes, and dispositions that have to do with one's loves. This kind of knowledge, the knowledge one lives by, is gained gradually over time. . . . The knowledge of God sinks into the mind and heart slowly and hence requires apprenticeship.[19]

We cannot reason our way to God without entrusting ourselves to others who know and love God. Those things that matter—God, humanity, and the world—are not learned without sympathy and enthusiasm, without giving of ourselves, and without a debt of love. The place where we must begin is with the persons whose lives are formed by the teaching, since Christian witness is inescapably bound to the witness of others, to a kind of seeing or knowing that is faith. "There is no way to Christ without *martyrs*, without witnesses."[20] In looking to Wesley as a credible witness of the gospel, my interest is similar to the view expressed by William Abraham:

John Wesley is not some norm of truth; nor is he a folk theologian waiting to be organized into a systematic theologian; nor is he merely our brother in the faith; nor is he a Doctor of the church; nor is he a prince of the church. He was and continues to be for many a spiritual Father in God. He was and is a minister of the gospel who has birthed us indirectly in the faith. He is a thinker and spiritual guide who has gone on to Glory and whose work, with all its shortsightedness and shortcomings, can still bring us to God and foster holiness of life and thought.[21]

The heart of Wesley's homiletic witness is oriented theologically, that is as a form of first order discourse that springs from and leads to a common life of devotion, doctrine, and discipline in which the Triune God is known and loved as the source and goal of all that is. For this reason, Wesley's homiletic witness is unintelligible apart from the ecclesial habits that gave shape to his faith, wisdom, and virtue as a lover of God and hearer of the Word. Or to put this differently, the renewal of our minds in God's image is enabled by the gifts of faith, hope, and love through which the Spirit reorients us to return to God the life we receive from God as a sacrifice of praise.

> This eternal life then commences when it pleases the Father to reveal the Son in our hearts; when we first know Christ, being enabled to "call him Lord by the Holy Ghost"; when we can testify, our conscience bearing us witness in the Holy Ghost, "the life I now live, I live by faith in the Son of God, who loved me, and gave himself for me." And then it is that happiness begins—real, solid, substantial. Then it is that heaven is opened in the soul, that the proper heavenly state commences, while the love of God, as loving us, is shed abroad in the heart, instantly producing love to all mankind; general pure benevolence, together with its genuine fruits, lowliness, meekness, patience, contentedness in every state; an entire, clear, full acquiescence in the whole will of God, enabling us to "rejoice evermore, and in everything give thanks."[22]

Because God is the primary speaker in preaching, bearing faithful witness *to* the gospel is inseparable from being transformed into a faithful witness *of* the gospel; a "partaker of the divine nature" in union with Christ through the sanctifying grace of the Holy Spirit (2 Peter 1:4). Richard Lischer underscores the importance of recovering the formation and holiness of a preacher for the practice of preaching.

> The person of the preacher is a good example of a topic that was of great importance for the medieval church but is now seldom discussed in homiletics. Most homiletic treatises from Augustine through the Middle Ages deal with the formation and holiness of the one appointed to preach. . . . Despite the interest in spirituality in both the church and popular culture today, however, one does not discern a revival of the classical preoccupation with the holiness of the preacher.[23]

The holiness of the preacher is intrinsic to the identity of the church as a people called forth and formed by the loving self-giving of the Father that is mediated by the Son through the work of the Spirit in the means of grace. This assumes, however, that homiletic excellence aims for congruence with the knowledge and love engendered by faith in the incarnate Word in whom the Spirit draws us into the Triune life. "In other words, prayer and preaching are inseparable, so that Christian speech is to be tested by the one work we have been given as God's creatures, which is the work of prayer."[24]

Contrary to contemporary "rationalists" (reason without revelation) or "enthusiasts" (revelation without reason), the substance and scope of Wesley's preaching was derived from neither opinion nor experience for attaining ends such as "changing the culture," "reaching people," or "meeting needs." Making Wesley "relevant" for evangelism and social activism "today" requires fitting him into the modern framework of theologies that either ignore or reject the world of trinitarian devotion, doctrine, and discipline that constituted his theology and ministry.[25] Rather than presuming Wesley's contemporary "irrelevance"—on terms established by the dogmatic certainties of "de-traditioned" liberal and conservative expressions of Christianity—we would do well to consider if our readings of Wesley have been shaped by

> the loss of a coherent experiment in theology [and I would add, in preaching] that bears any kind of robust continuity with Wesley. The great hymns are no longer sung; the fervent sacramentalism has been eroded; the robust orthodoxy has been undermined; the commitment to the poor has become a normative ideology; the evangelistic fervor has been sidelined; the biblical literacy has been lost; the official, canonical doctrines of the tradition are despised or idling; and the specific doctrines of new birth, assurance, perfection, and predestination are unknown or received with consternation.[26]

Although Wesley is well known as a popular preacher, he was not a typical popularizer who chose to omit aspects of the gospel for sermonizing that was adjusted to doing what "works." Transcending the popular wisdom of his day, Wesley's primary concern was spiritual and moral, both personal and social: that the credibility of living faith that bears visible, tangible fruit in a life of love, goodness, peace, and joy not be lost in such popular superficialities. Moreover, this commitment was sustained by a single-mindedness and simplicity of devotion that was grounded in the truth of the scriptural witness, illumined by the church's trinitarian faith, and nourished by the Spirit's empowerments through the ecclesial means of grace. Albert Outler writes:

> The gospel, in Wesleyan terms, is a joyous word from God to men, through men, in the depths of their existence. It speaks of their origins and ends—as God as ground and sustenance of their existence, of man as a divine experiment in moral freedom, of man's demoralization and sin, of God in Christ reconciling the world unto himself, and of the Holy Spirit at work in a community of maturing persons. The gospel is a word of man's reliance and hope in God, of God's imperative that men should love him without stint and their neighbors without self-interest. It is a call to repentance, conversion, new life. The gospel is an invitation from the Holy Spirit to fellowship in God's beloved community, in which men are inwardly moved to outward acts of thanksgiving, worship, and service.[27]

Of primary importance for Wesley is that the ministry of "preaching Christ" will entail an openness and vulnerability to the witness of the Holy Spirit who awakens repentance, bestows living faith, and inspires a life of holiness and good works toward God, others, and all creatures. In other words, preaching is theology, a kind of discourse through which the self-communication of the Father is appropriated by the Spirit's gifts of faith, hope, and love into a way of thinking, living, and speaking that is discerned and expressed with the "mind that was in Christ."

Writing in response to an inquirer, Wesley described the intimate relation between the truth of doctrine, preaching, and the Christian habits engendered by the new law of the gospel ruling in the heart and mind:

> I do preach to as many as desire to hear, every night and morning. You ask; what would I do with them; I would make them virtuous and happy, easy in themselves and useful to others. Whither would I lead them? To heaven; to God the Judge, the lover of all, and to Jesus the Mediator of the new covenant. What religion do I preach? The religion of love; the law of kindness brought to light by the gospel. What is this good for? To make all who receive it enjoy God and

themselves: to make them like God; lovers of all; contented in their lives; and crying out at their death, in calm assurance, "O grave, where is thy victory! Thanks be unto God, who giveth me the victory, through my Lord Jesus Christ."[28]

Shaped by an evangelical message and way of life within a catholic environment, or "evangelical catholicism," Wesley's public witness—as preacher, evangelist, pastor, and spiritual director—was at home within the church's calling to the perfection of love for God and neighbor, or holiness of heart and life. It is not surprising then, that Wesley's homiletic wisdom was not only shaped by preaching but also in praying, reading, writing, teaching, conversing, debating, communing, presiding, singing, organizing, visiting the sick, serving the poor, and ministering to prisoners. In all these activities, Wesley sought to perceive the reality of God's love ruling over, in, and through all things as the source and end of faith, piety, wisdom, virtue, and goodness.

For Wesley, then, the intelligibility of preaching is dependent upon the formation of a people who desire the goodness of the truth that is proclaimed; the gospel becoming a people. Commenting on the intimate relation between the Holy Spirit, the life of the church, the language of the Scripture, and the theological purpose of Christian speech, Charles Wood cites Wesley's reference to an assertion of Martin Luther, "Divinity is nothing but a grammar of the language of the Holy Ghost."

> The language of faith, or of the Christian community, is the language of people that bear that possibility in mind and who use their language in the hope that it may also be used by God. . . . Its [theology's] aim is to show how the language of faith may best fulfill its own aim, which is to serve as the language of the Holy Spirit, the language in which God judges us. . . . Of course it is precisely a familiarity with the historical and conventional language of the community, an immersion in it, that allows one to adapt it freely—like a native speaker who is able to respond sensitively and openly to the needs of a new context. . . . We make it our own just by exercising that ability to shape it to current needs.[29]

Unlike our time, when Christian doctrine and life are divided, Wesley understood theology as the saving wisdom revealed in Scripture that is made intelligible by the truth of Christian doctrine and made visible in a life of

Christian virtue through the means of grace. In other words, Wesley's attention and judgment were trained to hear Scripture as the living Word of God.

Assuming this union of doctrine and life, "good" preaching will presuppose the justifying and sanctifying activity of the Father that is mediated by the Son through the work of the Holy Spirit. On the other hand, if we assume knowledge of the Trinity is irrelevant to public life, the church will be shaped by godless images and debates about its ministry, including preaching, will be driven by utility and relevance, rather than the habits of mind that dispose us to hear the Word as the basis for speaking the truth in love.[30]

Methodist theologian Julian Hartt describes the church's calling to be a living embodiment of the gospel for which a preacher's life and speech serves as an exemplary witness:

> We have a great and desperate need for the gospel. The power of that word is not in utterance but in concrete life. The power of the word is that real, transcendently righteous and creative love. That alone is the power which can place us in solid and productive relationship to the real world. Hence, while the church has an utterance to make, sermons to preach, hymns to sing, and prayers to offer; above all it has a life to share. This life is God's free sharing of himself in Jesus Christ.[31]

A "Preaching Life"

As a member of the Wesleyan tradition, my thinking on the subject of the "preaching life" has been guided by an extended conversation with Wesley in relation to what he wrote of himself: "I do indeed live by preaching."[32] As a preacher, my hope has been to live more faithfully into our homiletic vocation by learning from Wesley the "preaching theologian." The largest part of this conversation with Wesley reflects my search for a deeper understanding of the "preaching life," which I would summarize in the following manner: becoming an exemplary witness of the gospel by which the Spirit calls and builds up the church to be a visible sign of God's kingdom through participation in the righteousness of Christ.

During more than sixty years of ministry and in excess of forty thousand sermons, Wesley's theology emerged from, and fed into, his preaching; a "kerygmatic theology" by which he sought to bear faithful witness to the gospel. Because it was not possible for Wesley to conceive of good preaching apart from the transformation of preachers by what is spoken, or of proclaiming "scriptural holiness" apart from faith in Christ that engenders love of God and neighbor through the gracious empowerments of the Spirit, it may also be fitting to say, "I indeed do preach by living."

For Wesley, Christian preaching was ordered by habits of the intellect, affect, and will by which the Spirit illumines the mind and enlivens the heart for speaking the truth in love. In other words, the character of the "preaching life" is inseparable from the gifts of faith, hope, and love by which the truth of God in Christ is received, lived, and proclaimed. As a means of grace, then preaching Christ engenders and is engendered by true religion, or the power of godliness; the love of God indwelling and filling the life of preachers and people through the presence and work of the Spirit. For Wesley, this is "true religion, even the whole mind which was also in Christ Jesus." He continues:

> There can be no doubt that but from this love to God and man a suitable conversation will follow. His "communication", that is, discourse, will "be always in grace, seasoned with salt", and meet to "minister grace to the hearers". He will always "open his mouth with wisdom", and there will be "in his tongue the law of kindness". Hence his affectionate words will "distil as the dew, and as the rain upon the tender herb". And men will know "it is not" he only "that speaks, but the Spirit of the Father that speaketh in him". His actions will spring from the same source as his words, even from the abundance of a loving heart.[33]

Such theologically informed and spiritually illumined practice makes Wesley a salutary exemplar of preaching that bears witness to the saving activity of the Father, Son, and Holy Spirit. Such humility cultivates the theological judgment required to discern that the things we do—evangelism, worship, and preaching—or the results we seek—"reaching people," "engaging the culture," or "transforming the world"—are not of greater importance than faith that comes by hearing and being formed by the Word into a life of love for God and others. In other words, the language and "grammar" of faith were still significant for Wesley in that preaching had not been reduced to a method or set of skills divorced from the work of Christ and the Holy Spirit through the means of grace.

On the other hand, for Wesley, evangelism that was not oriented toward transformation of the heart and life through participation in the righteousness of Christ would be seen as less than fully Christian. Left behind would be the convictions, habits, dispositions, and visible fruit of "true religion" that are cultivated through the public reading and hearing of the Scripture, confessing the truth of the creeds, participating in the liturgy and the Eucharist, adhering to the doctrine and discipline of the Anglican Church, and following the General Rules of Methodist Societies. As Outler comments, "The 'catholic substance' of Wesley's theology is the theme of participation—the idea that all is of grace and all grace is the mediation of Christ by the Holy Spirit."[34]

Evangelization, catechesis, and discipleship were means of hearing and receiving the truth of the Word through the presence and work of the Spirit. Preaching was the fruit of prayerful attention to God; public acclamations of praise for the extravagant love of the Father who sends the Son and Spirit to call, convert, and sanctify a people whose existence embodies the truth of God's mission in the world: "The link between this [evangelism] and doctrine is clear. It is in encounter with this gracious and deeply mysterious reality mediated in Word, sacrament, liturgy, and holiness that the church rediscovers the truths which lie buried in its doctrinal heritage."[35]

An eighteenth-century observer described the character of Wesley's life and "conversation" in the following manner,

> Today I learned for the first time to know Mr. John Wesley, so well known here in England, and called the spiritual Father of the so-called Methodists. He arrived home from his summer journey to Ireland, where he visited his people. He preached today at the forenoon service in the Methodist Chapel in Spitafield for an audience of more than 4,000 people. His text was Luke 1:68. The sermon was short but eminently evangelical. He has not great oratorical gifts, no outward appearance, but he speaks clear and pleasant. After the Holy Communion, which in all English Churches is held with closed doors at the end of the preaching service, when none but the Communicants are usually present, and which here was celebrated very orderly and pathetic. I went forward to shake hands with Mr. Wesley, who already . . . knew my name, and was received by him in his usual amiable and friendly way. He is a small, thin, old man, with his own and long and strait hair, and looks as the worst country

curate in Sweden, but has learning as a Bishop and zeal for the glory of God which is quite extraordinary. His talk is very agreeable, and his mild face and pious manner secure him the love of all rightminded men. He is the personification of piety, and he seems to me as a living representation of the loving Apostle John. The old man Wesley is already 66 years, but very lively and exceedingly industrious.[36]

Accounts such as this should not be dismissed as mere "hagiography," since it displays important elements of Wesley's life and work as a preacher that are instructive for us. As a "preaching theologian," Wesley displays a happy knowledge of God's justifying and sanctifying grace. Only God's abundant self-communication, mediated through the Son and the witness of the Spirit, is capable of engendering Christian speech that is characterized by knowledge, understanding, and discernment.[37] Wesley's intention was that ministers would cultivate such practical wisdom for calling others into the life of faith and holy living.

> O how can these who themselves know nothing aright, impart knowledge to others? How to instruct them in all the variety of duty; to God, their neighbor, and themselves? How will they guide them through the mazes of error, through all the entanglements of sin and temptation? How will he apprize them of the devices of Satan, and guard them against all the wisdom of the world?[38]

Wesley's practical wisdom invites us "back to the future" for cultivating a robust, trinitarian witness of preaching appropriate to the post-Christendom, missionary situation where we find ourselves.[39] As Long comments on this way of construing theology, "Rather than seeing this as a liability to be overcome by making [Wesley] relevant to our context, the irrelevance and alien character to [Wesley's] work may be what we need to help us see something other than the dogmatic certitudes of modernity."[40]

The strangeness of Wesley's work may indeed be his most important contribution in guiding us to see more clearly that the truth of God matters in every aspect of preaching. Wesley's homiletic wisdom does not assume the division of theology and practice, or homiletic content and form that continues to be perpetuated by both church and academy. Moreover, the importance of Wesley's work is not that it is so exceptional or unique in this regard but it matters because it is part of an important conversation about God and the moral life that he inherited from others and to which he made some faithful contributions. To be faithful to the Wesleyan tradition we should read and hear the witness of those others as much as we read and hear the witness of Wesley.[41]

Jaroslav Pelikan reminds us that the history of preaching holds a rightful and important place in the history of doctrine.[42] For this reason, Wesley's homiletic theology will remain in large part unintelligible to us unless we acknowledge his robust faith in the gracious initiative and providential action of the Triune God in the ministry of preaching and the lives of its participants. This vision of life and ministry was formed within a conversation that had "traditioned" him into the religion of the Bible and the life of holiness whose source and end is God.

For Wesley, then, theology is a practice that bears witness to the apostolic faith through preaching that seeks to assist the Spirit's work of calling and forming faithful followers of Jesus Christ. Following Wesley's own example, the following chapters take a longer view of things, examining his homiletic practice as an expression of Christian wisdom that was cultivated through the attentiveness of faith, the obedience of love, and the illuminating work of the Spirit. In other words, my intention in writing about Wesley is for the purpose of writing with him in order to illumine the theological orientation of his work for our time. This theological vision was derived from the heart of the apostolic message and mission: the truth of God which is heard, received, and handed down in a common life of doctrine, devotion, and discipleship.

In 1955, W. L. Doughty published *John Wesley: Preacher*, the only full-length study of Wesley's preaching.[43] Doughty's analysis is primarily literary in scope, dividing sermon texts into their constituent parts for the purpose of analyzing various aspects of homiletic theory and practice. Doughty's book provides an informative description of Wesley's preaching by means of discrete topics: a brief historical account of Wesley's background and preparation; Wesley's congregations; the effects of his preaching; positive response and resistance to his sermons; the style of his sermons; his manner of preaching; the themes of the sermons; his use of quotations and illustrations; concluding with the publication and preservation of the sermons.

Doughty's discussion does not call attention to the importance of Wesley's participation in a larger conversation related to theology, exegesis, and preaching. Nor does his work demonstrate how Wesley integrates these three divided modern "disciplines"—in the ministry of the Word for the purpose of making faithful followers of Jesus Christ. Rather, Doughty's categories divide Wesley's preaching into discrete parts that fail to take into account the larger, integrative vision that gave coherence to his theological convictions and pastoral practice. By dividing Wesley's sermons into their constitutive parts for the sake of homiletic analysis, Doughty's work overlooks the the practical wisdom that guides and characterizes Wesley's ministry. The following chapters take a different approach toward understanding Wesley as a "homiletic theologian" and exemplar of the preaching life.

Chapter Outlines

Chapter 1 provides a way into reading Wesley from the perspective of "practical wisdom," a form of "knowing in action," that integrates theology and practice in the truthfulness and goodness of the preacher. Chapter 2 explores what Albert Outler has described as Wesley's "baseline," the significant influence of Erasmus at the origins of the Anglican tradition. This Erasmian perspective, which joins faith and good works, helps us to understand more clearly Wesley's union of intellectual and moral virtue in devotion to God. Chapter 3 looks at Wesley's turn "back to the future" after Aldersgate; his serious engagement with the Church of England's *Book of Homilies* in discerning a homiletic theology for the emerging Wesleyan movement.

Chapter 4 examines Wesley's commitment to speaking "plain truth for plain people," in light of a long tradition of popular preaching in England. It shows that, contrary to pragmatic views of Wesley as a "popular" preacher, his primary concern in preaching was to discern and speak the truth of God. Chapter 5 discusses Wesley's interpretation of Scripture, which was inseparable from and expressed in his preaching. In other words, Wesley's exegesis *is* preaching; a participatory way of reading Scripture that overcomes the modern split of past and present, the world of Scripture and the world of those who read, speak, and listen. Chapter 6 picks up on a neglected emphasis in Wesley's understanding of salvation as our restoration to the divine image: happiness in

God. This is explored in conversation with two other significant preachers from the Christian tradition, Augustine and Thomas Aquinas. Their work helps to illumine the vision of salvation that was preached by Wesley: that through the presence and work of Christ and the Holy Spirit, the design and desire of God for human creatures are fulfilled in a common life of holiness and happiness. Finally, the conclusion summarizes the discoveries of the previous chapters to suggest ways that we might yet learn from Wesley as a homiletic theologian for whom the truth of God matters in a preacher's whole manner of thinking, living, and speaking.

CHAPTER 1

THE PRACTICE OF WISDOM

This book interprets Wesley as a preaching theologian who serves as an examplary witness to the task of assisting the work of the Holy Spirit in the ministry of the Word. It discusses the practical wisdom that characterized Wesley's preaching ministry in eighteenth-century England; a ministry that entailed a renewal and reintegration of Christian devotion, doctrine, and discipline. Contrary to much contemporary homiletic wisdom, the truth and goodness of Christian doctrine is relevant to neither evangelism nor the building up of Christian communities through the proclamation of the Word. Rather, knowing and loving the Triune God is necessary if the church is to be formed in the pattern of its crucified and risen Lord. In other words, the truth we know, love, and proclaim is embodied by faith in the activity of the Father through the Son who rules and indwells the church through the presence and work of the Holy Spirit.

Although the efficacy of preaching is dependent upon the voice of the risen Christ that is made audible by the work of the Holy Spirit, it will also include the participation of preachers who have been formed by the practical wisdom intrinsic to faith in the Word that works through love. In other words, the practical wisdom of preaching receives its shape in knowing and loving the truth and goodness embodied by Christ and the witness of Scripture, according to "the analogy of faith." This presumes, however, that the source and goal of preaching is love of God and neighbor—or holiness—that is the gift of the indwelling Spirit through which we know and bear witness to Christ and his work in our midst and in the world. Wesley writes:

> O who is able to describe such a messenger of God, faithfully executing his high office! Working together with God; with the great Author both of the old and the new creation! See his Lord, the eternal Son of God, going forth on that work of omnipotence, and creating heaven and earth by the breath of his mouth! See the servant whom he delighteth to honour; fulfilling the counsel of his will, and in his name speaking the word whereby is raised a new spiritual creation.[1]

For Wesley, "good" preaching is the good work of good preachers that participates in God's goodness by the grace of Jesus Christ through the witness of the Spirit. The source and goal of such "good" news is the Triune God who delights in communicating his goodness through an intensely intimate communion of love to redeem and renew creation.[2] Moreover, the redemption of God's good creation—viewed theologically as coming from God and returning to God—entails an "ecstatic" participation in Christ who orders the church's life through the Spirit's grace, gifts, blessings, and empowerments.[3]

Attending to Wesley in this manner will involve us in a conversation beginning with the early church and extending through the sixteenth-century for which theology—*theologia*—was a practical habit, or *habitus*, an aptitude of the intellect and will having the primary characteristic of knowledge seeking wisdom in love. In earlier times some saw this as a directly infused gift of God that was intimately tied to faith, prayer, virtue, and desire for God. Later, with the advent of formal theological investigation, others saw it as a form of wisdom that could also be promoted, deepened, and extended by human study and argument. However, the meaning of theology did not displace the more primary sense of the term; theology as a practical *habitus*, the habit of attending to God's saving wisdom in Christ through the work of the Holy Spirit in the worshiping life of the church.[4]

Theology, then, is a practical way of knowing which directs the mind and heart to God as the end of all human knowledge, desire, and action. This saving wisdom is mediated by the witness of Scripture in the ministry of the church through which the Spirit engenders faith that works through love of God, the neighbor, and all creatures in God. The mission of God is therefore acknowledged within a living tradition grounded in, and continuous with, the sending of Christ and the Spirit who call forth and create the church to embody the distinctive habits of "social holiness." Or as Bryan Stone writes:

> My point . . . is that Christian salvation is ecclesial—that its very shape in the world is a participation in Christ through worship, shared practices, disciplines, loyalties, and social patterns of his body, the church. To construe the message of the gospel in such a way as to hide what Christians called ecclesial is to miss the point of what God is up to in history—the calling forth and creation of a

people. The most evangelistic thing the church can do, therefore, is to be the church not merely in public but as a new and alternative public; not merely in society but as a new and distinct society, a new and unprecedented social existence. . . . "Social holiness," to use John Wesley's phrase, is both the aim and the intrinsic logic of evangelism.[5]

This theological and ecclesial perspective unites Wesley, the Oxford Don, and Wesley, the popular evangelist; two images that, if divided, betray a theory/practice split that perpetuates views of Wesley as either an irrelevant intellectual or anti-intellectual pragmatist. Dividing Christian doctrine and the Christian life, this modern dogma obscures the wisdom of Wesley's "practical divinity" in which the experience and ministry of the church was bound to and shaped by doctrinal convictions, just as theological understanding was grounded in and enriched by participation in the faith and life of the church.

Geoffrey Wainwright has summarized Wesley's integrity of vision and practice in the following manner:

> First, he looked to the Scriptures as the primary and abiding testimony to the redemptive work of God in Christ. Second, he was utterly committed to the ministry of evangelism, where the gospel was to be preached to every creature and needed only to be accepted in faith. Third, he valued with respect to the Christian Tradition and the doctrine of the Church a generous orthodoxy, wherein theological opinions might vary as long as they were consistent with the apostolic teaching. Fourth, he expected sanctification to show itself in the moral earnestness and loving deeds of the believers. Fifth, he manifested and encouraged a social concern that was directed toward the neediest of neighbors. Sixth, he found in the Lord's Supper a sacramental sign of the fellowship graciously bestowed by the Triune God and the responsive praise of those who will glorify God and enjoy him forever.[6]

Wesley approached the interpretation of Scripture as both an act of faith and means of grace through which the understanding and desire are engaged by the Word and the Spirit to induce the knowledge and love of God. He insisted that Methodist preachers engage in daily prayer and study for the purpose of nourishing faith, deepening understanding, and inspiring love—for God and neighbors in God—that enhances one's capacities for thinking, living, and speaking according to the "mind that was in Christ."[7] David Cunningham comments on the loss of such character in our time:

> The persuasive role of character was seriously devalued during the Enlightenment. The rise of experimental science emphasized the goal of neutrality, which was thought to be guaranteed only through radical detachment: subject and object were thus torn asunder. On this view, an experiment needed only to take place under properly controlled conditions; the character of the experimenter was irrelevant. Empirical experimentation tended to focus attention away from how things appear in nature, and toward exceptions to the rule. This narrow focus contributed to the reduction of the meaning of ethos from a complex, holistic *habitus* to a mere series of rules and regulations.[8]

Forgotten in this empirically derived view is that the goal of Christian faith, hope, and love is the restoration of the image of God in human creatures; an image that has been defaced but is now being restored by the Spirit through participation in the fellowship of the Father and the Son. "This renewal into the image of God takes place in the embodiment of a new law, which the Holy Spirit gives internally. This 'new law' is a participation in Christ's human righteousness where the Spirit sanctifies the believer."[9]

The life of Christian people, which includes preachers as exemplary witnesses, is the fruit of the new law of the gospel ruling the intellect, affect, and will through the grace of the Holy Spirit. Becoming a preacher entails cultivating capacities for discerning the truth and goodness of Christ through the illumination of the Spirit that engenders the knowledge we live by in the intellectual and moral virtues. Wesley writes:

> There can be no doubt that with this love to God and man a suitable conversation will follow. His "communication," that is, discourse, will "be always in grace, seasoned with salt," and meet to "minister grace to its hearers. " He will always "open his mouth with wisdom," and there will be "in his tongue the law of kindness." Hence his affectionate words will "distil as the dew, and as the rain upon the tender herb." And men will know "it is not" he only "that speaks, but the Spirit of the Father that speaketh in him." His actions will spring from the same source as his words, even from the abundance of a loving heart.[10]

The virtue of practical wisdom is committed to pursuing the good that is rooted in a definite community and tradition with favored character, dispositions, and habits. As a way of "knowing in action," practical wisdom, or prudence, is sustained by good character and habits that enable discernment of the good for the sake of doing good acts that are a source of joy. "The good practitioner has been formed by a history of participation in the practice itself. His or her experience of serving the end or *telos* of the practice—and recurrently trying to discover what this concretely requires—has laid down certain dispositions of character which, through discipline and direction, enable and energize."[11]

For this reason, a practically wise person will possess skills of deliberation, discernment, and decisiveness that make him or her capable of transforming knowledge of reality into virtuous speech and action. Michael Dauphinias and Matthew Levering describe practical wisdom, or prudence, in the following manner,

> Prudence not only includes making the right decision, but also demands we carry out the decision. In this way prudence links the intellectual and moral virtues (knowing and doing). Moreover, prudence shapes the other moral virtues insofar as it enables the just person to act justly, the courageous person to act bravely, and the temperate person to act with self-control.[12]

Joseph Dunne's discussion challenges an instrumentalist, "cause and effect" approach to practice that frames objectives in advance, anticipates plans, controls the moves one will make, and then evaluates both the activity and results on terms defined by "effectiveness."[13] Following the moral philosophy of Aristotle, Dunne argues persuasively that practice is irreducible to external techniques or procedures, but requires a nontechnical, personal, and participatory way of knowing that cannot be framed in terms of detachment, universality, and utility. This discussion shows that cause and effect utility, while presuming to be only "practical," actually embodies a definite kind of theory that is effectively reduced to mere skill and technique with no larger purpose or end.

Dunne defines this type of activity as a form of "making" that is specified by a maker who determines its end or goal in advance: "*Techne*, then, is the kind of knowledge possessed by an expert maker, it gives him a clear conception of the why and wherefore, the how and with what of the making process and enables him, through the capacity to offer a rational account of it, to preside over his activity with secure mastery."[14] In contrast to the activity of making or producing that proceeds by explanation, prediction, and control for acting externally upon the raw material of one's work, Dunne discusses the social activity of practice. A practice is conducted in public places in cooperation with others and with no ulterior purpose or goals external to sharing in the truth and goodness of the practice itself; and with a view to no other end or outcome than the moral intentions, habits, and qualities exemplified by wise, experienced participants of the practice.

This definition of shared communal activity may arguably be extended to Christian practices such as worship, the interpretation of the Scripture and preaching, evangelization, catechesis, training in discipleship, and pastoral care. Activities of this nature are carried out in such a way to realize and demonstrate their true end, those virtues, dispositions, and excellences valued by the church as a historical community and constitutive of its life and witness. This will require prudence, as Josef Pieper writes:

> Prudence, then, is the mold and mother of all the virtues, the circumspect and resolute shaping power of our minds which transforms knowledge of reality into realization of the good. It holds within itself the humility of silent; that is to say, of unbiased perception; the trueness—to—being of memory; the art of receiving counsel; alert, composed readiness for the unexpected. Prudence means the studied seriousness and, as it were, the filter of deliberation, and at the same time, the brave boldness to make final decisions. It means purity, straightforwardness, candor, and simplicity of character; it means standing superior to the utilitarian complexities of mere "tactics."[15]

Dunne interprets this kind of activity, that is *phronesis*, or practical knowledge, as a kind of "knowing how" that is historical, traditioned, personal, embodied, and shared with others. In other words, the wisdom of practice is as much a matter of who we are and to whom we belong as much as what we know.

In questioning the attainability of technical mastery over these areas an alternative to the technicist picture has been developed. In this alternative picture, practical knowledge has been shown as a fruit which can grow only in the soul of a person's experience and character; apart from cultivation of this soil, there is no artifice for making it available in a way that would count. In exposing oneself to the kind of experience and acquiring the kind of character that will yield requisite knowledge, one is not the kind of epistemic subject that has been canonized by the modern tradition of philosophy. One is at the same time a feeling, expressing, and acting person; and one's knowledge is inseparable from one as such.[16]

Dunne's description of these two distinct modes of activity can illumine how preaching articulates and embodies the practical wisdom that we are to love God and our neighbor as ourselves. Seen from this perspective, good preaching will be characterized by a particular kind of history, experience, judgment, and influence which, although rooted in the wisdom of Scripture and the Christian past, remains open to gifts, dispositions, and habits appropriate to hearing the Word and responding to the Spirit in the present.

Preaching, therefore, is a form of "ecstatic" speech that is enabled by the Holy Spirit through ongoing encounter with the living Word in worship, the sacraments, and the other means of grace. Thus when preaching is reduced to following "how to" steps—the procedural application of abstract, disembodied principles—its character is limited to technocratic knowledge possessed by an "expert" belonging to a specialized craft. What this will mean, however, is that the identity of "preacher" is defined as a person whose primary form of knowing consists of applying rules to effect results according to external criteria such as "relevance," "effectiveness," or "church growth." Stone comments:

> For if a practice [such as preaching] can be described and understood apart from the specifying ends (in other words, can be described in solely pragmatic terms), then one must ask whether the ends have been made external to the means, thereby disqualifying the practice as *practice*. Excellence is then determined by the efficacy of the activity in achieving or producing an assumed end rather than by the character of the practice itself embodying an end to which it is internally related.[17]

Craig Dykstra has commented extensively on a tendency toward reducing Christian practices to universalistic and abstract "one size fits all" procedures rather than the skills of living and speaking faithfully according to scriptural wisdom that is embodied by participatory, communal ways of knowing tested by the wisdom of God and the wisdom of the church. Dykstra's discussion parallels that of Dunne; that when practice is reduced to making something happen—a combination of knowledge, power, and the application of skills and techniques for producing desired outcomes and results—its nature will be understood technologically, individualistically, and ahistorically. What matters most in this kind of activity is the merely functional, which operates through cause-and-effect relations and is dependent upon its utility for attaining immediate ends—rather than convictions and virtues intrinsic to the church's faith, identity, tradition, and wisdom.[18]

Thus what is true or good and what is practical become separate issues; just as the faith of the preacher, the method of preaching, the content and context of preaching, are divided and treated as discrete, unrelated matters for the pursuit of "effectiveness." When this occurs, fidelity between speaker and words, language and truth, and language and deeds, are lost. Dykstra argues that this popular notion of practice, predicated upon effectiveness for production rather than excellence of the whole person, will in the end be left with no practice [and no practitioners]. If what practice that exists is reduced to mere technical routine or process with no point other than effecting change, it will exclude both the practice and participants from an ongoing history of knowledge, understanding, and love in which the distinctive truth, wisdom, and habits of the church and its way of life are handed down, received, and learned.[19]

The indispensability of prudence for the moral life provides an alternative to the popular vision of preacher as "Gnostic technician," since practical wisdom, as the fruit that grows in the soil of one's knowledge and love of God, is inseparable from the whole self as a thinking, feeling, expressing, and acting person. "In the end the guarantee of the trustworthiness of practical judgments and the validity of moral judgments lies not in any code but in the verdict of good, experienced, wise people."[20] Such practiced wisdom is not produced by a body of generalized knowledge, a set of principles and procedures, or a "method" is "applied" according to technical rationality and mastery for the "effective" achievement of predetermined outcomes. As Dunne states:

To speak of "action" as well as (but not separate from) knowledge and expression is to advert to the network of undertakings within one finds oneself—the unpredictability, open-endedness, and to the hazardousness of one's undertakings within this network—the unpredictability of what these undertakings set in train. No one is exempt from action in this sense (a sense which allows that speech often is action); it is through it that one discloses and achieves the unique identity that distinguishes one as a person; and at the same time it reveals the depth of one's interdependence with others. . . . When one's actions are not imposed on materials but are directed toward other persons . . . mastery is not attainable. One cannot determine in advance the efficacy of one's words and deeds.[21]

What we love plays a significant role in shaping our judgments. Love moves the intellect to engage in the process of practical reasoning and focuses the intellect's attention upon certain objects rather than others because of the intensity of its love.[22] For reason to discover the right act to be done, here and now, love in the will must be ordered wisely toward the practical good that is timely and appropriate. However, love ordered well will be directed toward God as its true end, while disordered love will be directed toward the self, to created things as their own ends, or as means to ends less than God. Prudence is akin to "love discerning well" with the power of the intellect working through practical judgment, counsel, and direction, an insightfulness which directs one's reason, desire, and actions to the end of love for and in God.[23]

Because prudence is "love choosing wisely," it is in the service of human excellence—loving the truth and desiring the good—which renders happy the person who knows, judges, speaks, and acts well.

> Prudence is a kind of practical wisdom receiving a new, profound light from faith and a higher strength from charity; which unites it to God and deepens its understanding of the neighbor. . . . Thus enlightened and penetrated, prudence becomes capable of fulfilling its role as director of action according to the designs of God. Its intervention is indispensable, because by means of prudence the theological virtues, like the others, can be embodied in concrete action. Without it, even charity could not discern and follow the right path with precision.[24]

There can be no wisdom or virtue without the gift of charity, since the goal of moral discernment is dependent upon knowing God through faith penetrated by love. Flowing from the will to the intellect, charity transforms prudence for knowing the right end and choosing the right means in conformity to that end. John Mahoney points out that the wisdom of the gospel and the illumination of the Spirit are the key elements of the New Law that inspired the prophets and apostles and moved the saints to act. Thus in addition to the union of heart and mind with God, the virtue of practical wisdom will require moral skills that enable assessment of specific situations and transformation of knowledge into appropriate action; for speaking or doing the right thing, for the right reason, in the right manner, for the right persons, and in the right circumstances.[25]

The mark of practical wisdom is a life ordered by love for God and the neighbor through prayer and the virtues. The virtue of faith grants knowledge of divine revelation as articulated by the articles of faith (the Creed) engendering the gift of wisdom that judges their truth according to God's self-giving in Christ. "The unfolding of doctrine in the practices of the church—for it is both a doing and a saying—serves to enfold the church into the very life of God. Thus all theology is finally mystical, a habit or "wisdom" given by the Spirit."[26] Moreover, the end of wisdom, as the gift that unites human being and acting, "is to let the primary action of God to spread out in us the divine being, the divine life."[27]

While the Holy Spirit bestows the gift of wisdom, the virtue of practical wisdom is indispensable for directing virtuous performances of the gospel that participate in, and are improvisations of, God's prior performance of the Word in Jesus Christ. The virtue of prudence thus lies at the heart of the preaching life, since without prudence we cannot speak in ways appropriate to becoming "holy performances." "Good" preaching, then, communicates God's goodness for the common good of the church that is dependent upon "a wisdom embodied in lives, practices and communities through the continual improvising of life in the Spirit shaped according to the 'mind of Christ.' "[28]

The preaching life, then, is shaped by the gift of wisdom that is received through attentiveness to Christ and the working of the Spirit's grace. "In other words, performance that is truly improvisatory requires the kind of attentiveness, attunement, and alertness traditionally associated with contemplative prayer. All of which is to say that the virtuoso is played even as she plays . . . likewise, language speaks the speaker as much as if not more than the speaker speaks the language."[29] Practicing such wisdom requires ingenuity, flexibility, and reliance upon an insightfulness that is immediate and intuitive, a way of "seeing" that is tested through long experience of patient decision making and good actions within the communion of love that is the church.[30] Father Romanus Cessario writes:

> Prudence aims at shaping the character of Christian believers so that they can fully participate in the communion of charity that abides in the Church. In the moral life of each person, the virtue of prudence must both conform and be conformed; prudence must be conformed to moral wisdom, i.e., to all the human intelligence can learn about a given subject. Prudence also learns from divine truth. In turn, prudence conforms to human behavior, so that human action lies . . . in accord with right direction that the ends or goods of human nature stipulate. Prudence brings us into right conformity with the "thing" or *res*, with reality as God knows the world to be.[31]

Practical wisdom requires the integration of human wisdom, virtue, and the will of God, the apprehension of an analogy between divine providence and the virtuous acts of prudent human beings.[32] Because the work of prudence puts right reason into emotion and desire, it is completed by judgment drawing from all the virtues to act as the "eyes and ears" of human excellence.[33] "The very grammar of faith points up to a vital sense in which theology is intrinsically performative. Word and deed are inseparable in the Christian life and practice; but since word and action will not always or completely coincide, Christians have always been concerned about "getting it right."[34] Pervading the whole of one's life, prudence is the capacity that judges rightly in uniting theological knowledge, love, and the activity of preaching, in virtuous performances of the gospel. As Fr. Chenu comments:

> Having these transcendent convictions and being empowered by its hope for eternal happiness, prudence still follows its appropriate means and keeps to its task and its functional orientation. Its efficacy remains bound up with the ways and means of its practical knowledge. Neither divine nor human love dismantles its ways of acting or its resources. The gospel moves through it.[35]

Thomas Aquinas's description of the relation between wisdom and prudence highlights the importance of the linkage between the Word of God, what is preached, the person who preaches, those to whom we preach, and the end(s) to which we preach.

> Since prudence concerns human affairs and wisdom, by contrast is concerned with the highest cause [God], it is not possible for prudence to be a greater virtue than wisdom. . . . Likewise Paul says, "The spiritual person judges everything and is judged by no one." So prudence does not get involved in the highest things which are the concern of wisdom, but rather governs matters that are subordinated to wisdom. In this way, prudence . . . is the servant of wisdom, because prudence prepares the way for wisdom a lot like the doorkeeper prepares the way for a king.[36]

Prudence, then, is neither a mechanical art nor a technical skill. Rather it is a capacity linking the intellectual and moral virtues for choosing good ends that are appropriate to a particular moral activity such as preaching (that is, receptivity to the Spirit's grace, attentiveness to and the praise of God, the gifts of faith, hope, and love, building up the body of Christ according to the law of the gospel) rather than external (that is, cultural relevance, pragmatic effectiveness, institutional self-promotion or preservation, a preacher's program or a particular social agenda). "The intellectual virtue of prudence is concerned with judging well among those means not only as effective for the end but also appropriate to me."[37]

"Good" preaching is the practice of knowledge that is cultivated by receptivity to God's incarnate Wisdom revealed in the apostolic witness to Christ; a nonutilitarian way of speaking that awakens the church to faith and love to God in ways that are timely and appropriate to building up the body of Christ.

The collaboration of charity and prudence works to integrate one's thoughts, affections, and actions for imitating the second person of the Trinity, the incarnate Wisdom of God.[38] Governed by prudence, the knowledge of faith is transformed into fitting performances of the Word through human speech that turns both preacher and listeners to the One who is the source and end of all our actions and words. Thomas Hibbs writes:

There is an inescapable reciprocity between understanding and loving in the Christian conception of the good life. Although the virtue of faith resides in the intellect, the object of faith is simultaneously the first truth of the good that is the "end of all desires and actions." . . . The reciprocity of contemplation and action is also evident in the connection between the theological virtues and the gifts of the Holy Spirit. The goal is union with a personal God. . . . The intimate connection between charity and the gift of wisdom is instructive. The gift of wisdom is the fruit of charity. . . . It empowers us to conduct life in light of divine truth. . . . Like prudence charity efficaciously orders the whole of human life and integrates cognition and affection.[39]

As a Christian practice, preaching is attentive to and affected by the presence of Christ constituting the church as his body through the work of the Holy Spirit. In other words, the practical wisdom of preaching is engendered by divine grace that works through the virtues of faith, hope, and love to enable judgment and discernment for speaking "to the right person, to the right extent, at the right time, with the right aim, and in the right way." Or as Wesley writes: "the love of God and man not only filling my heart, but shining through my whole conversation."[40] Dunne concludes that such wisdom and virtue requires a form of kenosis, or self-emptying,

> divesting itself of godlike notions and coming to accept that it cannot have and therefore must no longer aspire to a god's eye view for the human condition. And this movement away from detachment, sovereignty, and imperturbability has at the same time been a movement into and a taking upon itself the burdens of finitude, contingency, and situatedness. In subverting the Cartesian subject, it has been reincarnating the real person in the world of history and language, actions and involvement with other people—and, of course, in his/her own affective and bodily being.[41]

In the sermon "The Circumcision of the Heart," Wesley writes of the particular kind of self-emptying or humility that will be required if we are to see as God sees; with the eyes of the heart and understanding illumined by the "mind of Christ" that was embodied in his obedience of love to the Father.

> In general we may observe it is that habitual disposition of soul which in the Sacred Writings is termed "holiness," and which directly implies the being

cleansed from sin, "from all filthiness of both flesh and spirit," and by consequence of being endued with those virtues which were also in Christ Jesus, the
being so "renewed in the image of your mind" as to be "perfect, as our Father in
heaven is perfect." . . . This is that lowliness of mind which they have learned
of Christ who follow his example and tread in his steps. And this knowledge
of their disease, where by they are more and more cleansed from one part of
it, pride and vanity, disposes them to embrace a willing mind the second
thing implied in "circumcision of the heart"—that faith which alone is able to
make them whole, which is the one medicine given under heaven to heal their
sickness.[42]

An example of Wesley's practical wisdom is evinced by a letter he wrote in
December 1751, when the spread of evangelical revival was provoking both
enthusiasm and resistance. Wesley wrote to an inquirer on the subject of
"preaching Christ," presumably after pondering this matter for a period of
three months.[43] His description of "preaching Christ" is both theological and
pastoral in scope and provides a summary of God's mission—the love of God
for sinners demonstrated in the life, death, resurrection, and intercession of
Christ and his blessings—and the law setting forth the commands of Christ,
and in particular, the Sermon on the Mount.

This practical vision was cultivated by Wesley's study of Scripture and intimate knowledge of the Christian life. Revealing his theological and pastoral
understanding of the relation between the law and the gospel, his comments
reflect the practical judgment that is required to address a wide range of spiritual and moral conditions, including that of sinners, the justified, the diligent,
the proud, the careless, and the weak in understanding.[44]

Wesley directs particular attention to Methodist preacher John Wheatley,
whom he describes as a "gospel preacher" and "neither clear nor sound in the
faith." According to Wesley, Wheatley's sermons had the sound of "an uncon-
nected rhapsody of unmeaning words" and "Verses, smooth and soft as cream,
in which was neither depth nor stream."[45] Wesley was concerned with the
effects of "gospel" preaching, which despite its rhetorical finesse and popular
appeal, lacked both theological coherence and moral wisdom. Long on
promises and short on commands, it corrupted hearers, vitiated their taste,
ruined their desire for sound teaching, and spoiled their spiritual appetites,

feeding them "sweetmeats" until the genuine wine of the kingdom seemed insipid. Wesley concluded that while such popular "gospel preachers" were adept at attracting and pleasing large crowds, their preaching was characterized by "cordial upon cordial" that destroyed listeners' capacities for retaining and digesting the pure milk of the Word.[46]

On the other hand, the Methodist manner of preaching provided a practical wisdom for construing both law and gospel in light of the truth of Christ through the work of the Spirit who calls and creates a people in the knowledge and love of God. Wesley states:

> At our first beginning to preach at any place, after a general declaration of the love of God to sinners, and his willingness that they should be saved, to preach the law, in the strongest, the closest, the most searching manner possible; only intermixing the gospel here and there, and showing it, as it were, afar off. After more and more persons are convinced of sin, we may mix more and more of the gospel in order to "beget faith," to rein into spiritual life those whom the law hath slain; but is not to be done too hastily either.[47]

Wesley sketches a brief order of salvation in which one is drawn, converted, and led by the teaching of the law to living faith in the saving activity of Christ through which the Spirit bears the fruit of good works and holiness. "God loves you; therefore, love and obey him. Christ died for you; therefore, die to sin. Christ is risen; therefore, rise in the image of God. Christ liveth forevermore; therefore, live to God, till you live with him in glory."[48]

A sermon from the same year, "The Law Established by Faith II," states this more fully:

> It is our part thus to "preach Christ" by preaching all things whatsoever he hath revealed. We may indeed, without blame, yea, and with a peculiar blessing from God, declare the love of our Lord Jesus Christ. We may speak in a more especial manner, of "the Lord our righteousness" [Jer. 23:6], we may expatiate upon the grace of God "reconciling the world unto himself" [2 Cor. 5:19]; we may, at proper opportunities, dwell upon his praise, as bearing the "iniquities of us all," as "wounded for our transgressions" and "bruised for our iniquities," that "by his stripes we might be healed" [Is. 53:4–5]. But still we should not preach Christ according to his Word if we would wholly confine ourselves to this. We are not

ourselves clear before God, unless we proclaim him in all his offices. To preach Christ as a workman that needeth not be ashamed [2 Tim. 2:15] is to preach him not only as our great "High Priest, taken from among men, and ordained for men, in things pertaining to God"; [Heb. 5:1], as such "reconciling us by his blood" [Rom. 5:9, 10], and "ever living to make intercession for us" [Heb. 7:25], but likewise as the Prophet of the Lord, "who of God is made unto us wisdom" [1 Cor. 1:30], who, by his word and his Spirit, "is with us always, guiding us into all truth" [Jn. 16:13]; yea, and as remaining a King for ever, as giving laws to all whom he has bought with his blood, as restoring those to the image of God whom he had first reinstated in his favour, as reigning in all believing hearts until he "subdued all things to himself" [Phil. 3:21], until he hath utterly cast out all sin, and "brought in everlasting righteousness" [Dan. 9:24].[49]

Wesley's doctrinally informed, evangelically oriented preaching—"plain truth for plain people"—articulated the gospel as the wisdom and power of God. Such preaching evoked new conversions and fresh returnings; penitent responses to the promptings of the Spirit that were communicated by joyful witness to Christ and nurtured into disciplined love for God and neighbor within a common life of grace. The gift of living faith in love and the fruit of good works was evinced in a wide range of circumstances, but especially among the poorest and most humble of circumstances and conditions where God's generosity, love, and goodness were gladly received. Bearing witness to surprising manifestations of divine grace, such communal remembrances of God's redemptive work evoked robust, energetic, outpourings of "wonder, love and praise" that called attention to their source and goal: the praise of the Triune God who forgives, reconciles, and restores human creatures to the divine image.[50]

These startling acts of conversion, growth, and social witness were not seen as the result of choosing the right homiletic method or using the most effective evangelistic technique, but rather were viewed as forms of concrete, visible witness—in both their initial workings and maturing fruit—pointing to the joy of knowing and loving God, or "one thing needful." Wesley articulated this practical wisdom in his sermon, "The New Creation," demonstrating a proper relation between the goods of creation and the final good that is God.

The one perfect good shall be your ultimate end. One thing shall ye desire for its own sake—the fruition of him who that is all in all. One happiness ye shall propose to your souls, even a union with him that made them, the having fellowship with the Father and the Son, the being "joined to the Lord in one Spirit." One design ye are to pursue to the end of time—the enjoyment of God in time and eternity. Desire other things so far as they tend to this. Love the creature—as it leads to the Creator. But in every step you take be this, the glorious point that terminates your view. Let every affection, and desire or fear, whatever ye seek or shun, whatever ye think, speak, or do, be in order to your happiness in God, the sole end as well as the source of your being. Have no end, no ultimate end, but God. Thus our Lord: "One thing needful."[51]

Wesley's homiletic wisdom points to a "grammar" of faith that is ordered by knowledge and by love.[52] Such practical wisdom entails a participation in Christ's human righteousness; having the "mind that was in Christ" through which the Spirit transforms and guides our thinking, living, and speaking by the law of the gospel ruling in the mind and heart.[53] As he writes:

Prudence (or practical wisdom), properly so called, is not that offspring of hell which the world calls prudence, which is mere craft, cunning dissimulation; but . . . that "wisdom from above" which our Lord peculiarily recommends to all who would promote his kingdom upon earth. . . . This wisdom will instruct you how to suit your words and whole behavior to the persons with whom you have to do, to the time, place, and all other circumstances.[54]

In "An Address to the Clergy," Wesley writes of the need to be zealous in doing good and careful to abstain from evil. He describes the kind of practical wisdom required for guiding others to be discerning in the life of faith.

Have I any knowledge of the world? Have I studied men (as well as books) and observed their tempers, maxims, and manners? Have I learned to be beware of men; to add the wisdom of the serpent to innocence of the dove? Has God given me by nature, or have I acquired, any measure of the discernment of spirits; or of its near ally, prudence, enabling me on all occasions to consider all circumstances, and to suit and vary my behaviour according to the various combinations of them? . . . And do I omit no means which is in my power, and consistent with my character, of "pleasing all men" with whom I converse, "for their good to edification?"[55]

Preaching the gospel is inseparable from the sense that a preacher's vocation consists in making the truth and goodness of Christ her own. This is not possible unless the love of God is the controlling passion of one's life and ministry; a desire that the eyes of the heart be purified to see God's truth and goodness in all things. Wesley gives this practical wisdom a christological interpretation.

Do all who have spiritual discernment take knowledge (judging of the tree by its fruits) that "the life which I now live, I live by faith in the Son of God"; and that in all "simplicity and godly sincerity I have my conversation in the world"? Am I exemplarily pure from all worldly desire, from all vile and vain affections? Is my life one continued labour of love, one tract of praising God and helping man? Do I in everything see "Him who is invisible"? and "beholding with open face the glory of the Lord," am I "changed into the same image from glory to glory, by the Spirit of the Lord"?[56]

CHAPTER 2

LEARNING AND DEVOTION

The work of Alisdair MacIntyre reminds us that Christian practices such as preaching are embedded in historical communities and demonstrated by exemplars possessing appropriate wisdom and virtue for the continued excellence of the craft.[1] This is especially significant in light of the sacrament of baptism in which the Holy Spirit incorporates us into "the living faith of the dead,"[2] thereby teaching us to be wise interpreters of the Scripture, truthful speakers of the gospel, and faithful disciples of the Lord whom we confess, love, and obey. Rather than directing exclusive attention to "the experience of contemporary and socially privileged observers over all other human experience," we would do well to consider the wisdom of the saints, from among whom Wesley serves as an exemplary witness of the gospel that is able to empower living faith and holiness.[3] Wesley described witness as a form of practical wisdom that is patterned after Christ and enlivened by the Spirit:

> O who is able to describe such a messenger of God, faithfully executing his high office! Working together with God; with the great Author both of the old and the new creation! See his Lord, the eternal Son of God, going forth on that work of omnipotence, and creating heaven and earth by the breath of his mouth! See the servant whom he delighteth to honour; fulfilling the counsel of his will, and in his name speaking the word whereby is raised a new spiritual creation.[4]

The preaching of the gospel is generated by the presence and work of Christ and of the Holy Spirit, transforming both preachers and listeners into a corporate sign and instrument of God's mission, the *missio Dei*, in the world.[5] For Wesley, the subject of "practical divinity" is the trinitarian doctrine of God's salvation in Christ that emerges from, and feeds back into, the proclamation of the gospel.[6] As a priest of the Church of England and the reluctant leader of a movement that sought its evangelical reform, Wesley was "traditioned" into the life of the church within a practical context of Scripture, the confession of doctrine, the liturgy and sacraments, and works of piety and mercy; the means of grace through which the Spirit creates a holy people across time.[7] In many ways, Methodism was a consequence of reform that began in England at the turn of the sixteenth century, serving as a renewing force in parishes, working with common pastoral aims, participating in an educational and missional endeavor that underwrote the dissemination and transmission of evangelical faith and life.[8] Albert Outler writes:

> In the Methodist traditions after his death . . . the rationalists of the Enlightenment discounted tradition, experience, and even Scripture, save where it squared with their reading of right reason. Romantics and pietists discounted tradition and reason, except for the purpose of polemics, and turned to experience as their touchstone for Christian truth, including the truths of Scripture. . . . And yet, one cannot point to another theologian in the eighteenth century with a stronger sense of tradition, in a very broad sense, or whose popular theology was more heavily influenced by what he had learned from his Christian ancestors, both immediate and remote.[9]

For Wesley, learning to hear and speak the Word was situated within a common life of doctrine, devotion, and discipleship that is handed down, sustained, and renewed in and through communities of confession and praise: the confession of the Triune God's truth and goodness as the source and end of all things; the praise of the Triune God who communicates his truth and goodness in creating and redeeming all things. It is significant, then, that the English reformers maintained a robust commitment to the Trinity who affirmed the Apostles', Nicene, and Athanasian creeds. Moreover, the *Book of Common Prayer* is itself pervaded by trinitarian discourse for use in liturgical settings for the purpose of shaping a vision of God's saving activity that leads to the joy of communion with the living God.[10] In other words, by coming to know and love God within the economy of salvation, worshipers are made participants in the Triune life and mystery.

It is also important to note that the Anglican Thirty-Nine Articles of Religion speak about Scripture only after confessing faith in the Trinity, the incarnate Word, and the ministry of salvation through Christ and the Holy

Spirit. The church's relationship to the Triune God is primary for arriving at a view of Scripture as an instrument of salvation through which Christ and the Holy Spirit affect faith that bears fruit in good works and holiness of life. Rather than beginning with the apologetic arguments of Protestant scholasticism, Wesley affirmed that Holy Scripture speaks through the Spirit's testimony to foster communion with the Triune God. In other words, Holy Scripture functions "sacramentally," or as a means of grace, mediating Christ and the fullness of his saving work through the "oracles of God."[11] The primary aim of preaching, then, is assisting the Spirit's work of making and building up Christians through attentiveness to the Word of God in the words of Scripture.

In a sermon during the latter years of his ministry, Wesley asks, "What is Methodism? What does this new word mean? Is it not a new religion? Methodism, so called, is the old religion, the religion of the Bible, the religion of the primitive church, the religion of the Church of England." He goes on to define this more clearly:

> And this is the religion of the Church of England, as appears from all her authentic records, from the uniform tenor of her liturgy, and from number less passages in her Homilies. . . . The scriptural primitive religion of love, which is not reviving throughout the three kingdoms . . . is beautifully summed up in that one comprehensive petition, "Cleanse the thoughts of our hearts by the inspiration of thy Holy Spirit, that we may perfectly love thee, and worthily magnify thy holy name."[12]

Wesley's practical wisdom was grounded in the larger framework of the Christian tradition as it developed in Anglicanism. Viewed from the perspective of this tradition, Methodism is best understood as an orthodox, evangelical, and sacramental movement nourished by the ministry of the Word and celebration of the Eucharist, a "high church evangelicalism" oriented to knowing and loving the Triune God.[13] Albert Outler makes an important point regarding Wesley's theological interests, practice, and self-understanding that deserves further consideration.

> It is important to begin with the recognition that Wesley's baseline was Erasmian, as this particular perspective had been shaped through the course of

the English Reformation. . . . This tradition involved a sincere commitment to the ideals of Christian humanism (non-dogmatic in mood and style), open to an alliance between reverent faith and reverent learning, concerned above all with a gracious Christian lifestyle.[14]

Erasmus and the Unity of Faith, Learning, and Life

The academic and pastoral contributions of Erasmus of Rotterdam (d. 1536), who was a visiting scholar at Cambridge University during the reign of Henry VIII, were significant in shaping a generation of preachers, church leaders, and scholars who participated in the renewal and reform of the church in England.[15] Like Luther and Calvin on the Continent, Erasmus desired to rejuvenate and reform Christianity through a reclaiming of the power of speech. However, he is a foundational figure whose spiritual vision and intellectual insight are often overlooked in the story of reformation in England. At the origins of Anglicanism in its Protestant form, Erasmus' *Paraphrases on the New Testament*, along with the *Great Bible*, the *Book of Homilies*, and the *Book of Common Prayer* were required by royal injunction to be placed in churches for the education of clergy and laity. Significantly, the spirit and substance of Erasmian reform united faith and good works in devotion to God to supply the English Reformers with a distinctive way of integrating theology and practice within the church's life. Richard Schoeck asserts, "In studying the thought and letters of Tudor England one cannot ignore the presence of Erasmus and the centrality of Erasmian Humanism, and it would be difficult to overstate the importance of that influence."[16]

Religious and intellectual change in England during the early sixteenth-century had stirred an increasing desire for biblically inspired personal regeneration and social change.[17] The influence of Erasmus at Cambridge University—in the form of Christian humanism—a return to biblical scholarship, especially the New Testament, and an attachment to the Church Fathers and classical learning, stimulated a quantum leap in the importance of studying Scripture for its use in preaching and the renovation of the late medieval church.[18] As a consequence, proclaiming the word of God was the primary objective toward which all other intellectual and spiritual concerns were subordinated.[19]

During the past thirty years there has been a shift away from certain traditional interpretations of Erasmus, a bias shared by both Protestants and Catholics that has viewed him as a skeptic, indifferent or hostile to doctrine, a rationalist, and a precursor of Enlightenment.[20] Hilmar Pabil argues that we must not overlook the main purpose of Erasmus' religious work, namely the teaching and practice of piety (*pietas*) that shaped a synthesis between theology and spirituality. Erasmus' interests were not directed toward writing theological books in the mode of late medieval scholastic discourse. Rather, like a good preacher and evangelist his desire was to awaken contemporaries from their spiritual slumbers for a life of prayer and study that would engender love of God through faith in Christ and his *philosophia*—faith working through love.[21]

John O'Malley describes Erasmus' piety as pastoral in nature and scope: that nothing is more characteristic of Erasmus than his striving to reunite sound learning with godly living for their completion in the work of pastoral ministry: "Piety, theology and ministry were for him but different aspects of the one reality." Erasmus' piety was corrective, reforming, and in large part, an alternative in comparison with much that was around him. His goal was to use the past as an instrument to correct, rather than confirm, the present in continuity with the patristic and medieval spiritual traditions.[22] As Erasmus communicated to Pope Leo X, "To restore great things is sometimes not only harder but a nobler task than to have introduced them."[23] Erasmus occupied a moderating position that cultivated both a Catholic sense for the traditional development of doctrine and a Protestant critique of tradition on the basis of the once-and-for-all evangelical standard. He supported neither radical reformers nor Catholic theologians who were inclined to use the gospel to justify the status quo of ecclesiastical tradition and practice.[24]

Seen within the context of "Christian humanism," this practical wisdom was christological in character. In other words, the content of Erasmus' theology was characterized by emphasis on the incarnate Word and human words as mediating between God and listeners who are made to be born again, to grow up, and to move on to perfection. The "philosophy of Christ," a term lovingly embraced by the Church Fathers, denotes living faith in Christ based on centrality of the Word and the affective, participatory nature of the Christian life. Taken as whole, Erasmus' doctrinal commitments were uncontroversial, holding to the consensus of the Christian tradition; the doctrine set forth in the Scripture, the creeds, and the early councils of the church. This orthodox doctrinal vision centered on faith in Christ, the Christian life, and the church as the body of Christ. For Erasmus, then, theology is truly theology when it dwells in human hearts, words, actions and prayers in response to the activity of Christ through the presence and work of the Holy Spirit. Such practical virtues emerged from and were nourished by learning and devotion that aimed to unite doctrine and life, grace and nature, theological commitments inseparable from a particular kind of people and the distinctive practices that constitute their life.[25]

Arguably, Erasmus' greatest contribution as a teacher was his commitment to the centrality of the Word through the study of grammar, rhetoric, and philology—Greek, Latin, and Hebrew—to train preachers who would spread the teaching of the gospel and its way of life. A theologian will be a student of the Scripture, theology a form of wisdom, and wisdom a means of true religion: love for God and neighbor. Uniting the study of the Scripture and doctrine with practicing the Christian life, theology cultivates prudent, discerning hearts to explicate the Scripture, to speak movingly of love and devotion to God, and to stir passion for the things of God. Erasmus therefore sought to convey the spiritual and moral virtues he hoped would be cultivated to form devout, learned pastors competent to preach from the holy page of the Scripture. To this end he sought to provide a model of clear scriptural faith for which the piety, wisdom, and eloquence of the Church Fathers were better and more fruitful than the arid, complex, and proud disputations of late medieval schoolmen whom he perceived as contributing to malpractice in pastoral ministry and preaching.[26]

The work of Rowan Greer demonstrates that the early church maintained a steady conversation between theology and the life of the church. Those who were charged with elaborating technical theology were also preachers in the church whose aim was to articulate and shape the experience of ordinary Christians. For this reason doctrine and life were one. The church's worship was not simply an appropriation of the past but a present, corporate experience of God articulated by the church's faith. The preacher's task was to put into words the wisdom of what the church was being given to apprehend and know: its present appropriation of the Savior and his saving work in the world.[27] As a Christian practice, preaching is a primary medium through which the church articulates and enacts its vision of the gospel in tangible form.

Greer's discussion of the intimate connection of theology and life in the early church helps to illumine the separation of theology and practice, or content and form, which Erasmus hoped to overcome. According to patristic wisdom, Christian lives are the best apology for the truth of the gospel, or doctrine come to life. In Erasmus' time, these divisions had contributed to a separation of theological convictions and the life of the church so that much pastoral and church practice remained untested by Christian wisdom, and much Christian wisdom was uninformed by pastoral and ecclesial practice. However, faithful preaching of the gospel requires a reconciliation of theology and practice that is demonstrated by truthful witness to Christ and manifested by the concrete reality of the church: "The Christian vision is meant to be translated into virtue: the faith that apprehends God's gratuitous forgiveness in Christ must be translated into radical obedience to him."[28]

Writing to a fellow pastor in November 1519, Erasmus offers a clear summary of this vision:

> Besides which the whole of Christian philosophy lies in this, our understanding that all our hope is placed in God, who freely gives us all things through Jesus his Son, that we were redeemed by his death and engrafted through baptism with his body, that we might be dead to the desires of this world and live by his teaching and example, not merely harbouring no evil by deserving well of all men; so that, if adversity befall, we may bear it bravely in hope of the future reward which beyond question awaits all good men at Christ's coming, and that we may ever advance from one virtue to another, yet in such a way that we claim nothing for ourselves, but ascribe any good we do to God.[29]

Erasmus viewed himself as a steward of Christ's philosophy, as practicing the cure of souls by accommodating to their lives and for their benefit the wisdom of Scripture that nurtures authentic Christian faith and fruit.[30] Because the interpretation of Scripture will require both theological insight and pastoral discernment, a preacher must consider not only what is said but also by whom and to whom it is said, and with which words and how, at what time, on what occasion, and what preceded and followed it. In spreading *docta pietas* (learned piety) through the written word, Erasmus served as an exemplar of such practical wisdom by teaching the gospel to convert and transform his readers, and through their ministry, the people to whom they preached.[31]

In March 1516, Erasmus published the long-awaited *Novum Testamentum*, directing considerable attention to the subject of Scripture and its importance for the church.[32] It consisted of a dedication, followed by preliminary matters, the *Paraclesis, Methodus,* and *Apologia,* respectively a persuasive appeal to read the New Testament, guides for its use, and a defense of the undertaking. Erasmus himself provided the Greek text with a Latin translation. Finally came the *Annotations,* notes on the text, which take up almost as much space as the Latin and Greek texts put together. The introductory material pleads for a theology that would start with the words and concepts of Scripture to promote the use of biblical language as an instrument for overcoming the division between Christian teaching and the Christian life. As he wrote of how he often felt while listening to a sermon, "I see how simple people, who hang open-mouthed on the lips of the preacher, yearn for food for the soul, eager to learn how they can go home better people."[33]

In his introductory letter to readers, Erasmus explained how he produced the work, describing it as "the humblest service in pious devotion," and "a work of piety, a Christian work." His purpose was to render Scripture more eloquent, lucid, and faithful to the discourse of the apostles, offering Christ and inviting more followers to his wisdom by taking up a life of faith and love. This is repeated in the dedicatory letter to Pope Leo X, whom Erasmus addressed as "a second Esdras, a re-builder of the Christian religion" to whom he offered the *Novum Instrumentum* as a gift for the daily advancement of the Christian life.[34]

Erasmus chose the title *Instrumentum,* which may mean organ, instrument, or means of teaching and writing.[35] His purified text of the New Testament was to serve as an instrument for the wisdom of Christ, the human speech of the Father who is revealed in Scripture. A controversial expression of its rhetorical purpose appeared in the 1519 edition, the *Novum Testamentum*, which rendered the translation of John 1:1, "In the beginning was the Word" as *sermo* rather than *verbum*, meaning not simply words uttered singly but discourse that is copious, eloquent, and meaningful. Christ is the sermon of God, divine wisdom incarnate who in the writings of the evangelists and apostles "still lives and breathes for us and acts and speaks with more immediate efficacy than any other way." In other words, Holy Scripture speaks to effect what it says.

According to Erasmus, the sacred text is replete with the authority of God and alive with the presence of Christ, the transcendent and transforming Word who speaks through human words.[36] Erasmus' hope was that homiletic theologians trained in the disciplines of exegesis and rhetoric, with the guidance of Christ's wisdom and the empowerments of the Spirit, would proclaim the Word with passion to enkindle desire for the gospel. Because education and formation are inseparable, the knowledge and love of God that suffuses a preacher's life is able to pass into the hearts and minds of receptive listeners. As God's Wisdom incarnate, Christ unites the content and form of preaching; as God's human speech, Christ authorizes and empowers homiletic performance of the Word. Hoffman notes, "Erasmus wished for the church's external means of grace to operate according to their spiritual purpose. This pertains in particular to the ministry of proclaiming God's word incarnate in Christ and the Scripture."[37]

Erasmus viewed his biblical scholarship as an instrument of the transforming wisdom and power of Christ and therefore capable of restoring the unique sacramental meaning of the word of revelation. This purpose is articulated in the *Paraclesis*, the classic statement of his evangelical humanism.[38] Written in the form of a doxological hymn of praise to the philosophy of Christ, the *Paraclesis*, or word of exhortation, appeals to Christians to interpret Scripture with the desire to be formed into its saving wisdom.[39] Although Erasmus wrote his short "trumpet blast" to address a general readership, its startling force was particularly felt by preachers, generating an immediate response that anticipated its eventual popularity among Protestants who were drawn to its strong emphasis on God speaking through the medium of Scripture.[40]

Erasmus claimed that Holy Scripture, as the oracles of God, when interpreted in a manner appropriate to its subject matter, is capable of speaking with sufficient persuasiveness to accomplish its spiritual purpose: rendering the living mind and image of Christ who draws readers and listeners into the transforming wisdom of divine love. This requires language appropriate to its sacred subject, even if less ornate than sophistry that aims primarily to stimulate pleasure and delight. In contrast to the fleeting futility of classical oratory, scriptural eloquence renders the wisdom of Christ that "not only captivates the ear, but which leaves a lasting sting in the minds of its hearers, which grips, which transforms, which sends away a far different listener than it received." Because Scripture restores our capacity for responding to God, its appeal is primarily affective, moral, and transformative, engaging both the understanding and desire.[41]

When the word of Scripture is spoken without the hindrance of human foolishness, the Spirit is free to inflame and incite human hearts that sing Christ's praise.[42] Erasmus saw Christian people everywhere for whom the word of Christ had been muted and even silenced by theological ignorance and lukewarm piety. The *Paraclesis* thus offered a compelling summons to acquire new capacities within a divine-human conversation, an invitation to a transformed life consisting of faith and love through the work of Christ that is accompanied by the Spirit. Marjorie O' Rourke Boyle comments:

> Rhetoric seeks an act of the will, assent, and secures its religious end in conversion. . . . A particular efficacy of rhetoric toward this transformation defines it as the language of the Spirit Christ spoke. Rhetoric is unitive. So is the Spirit. It is the Spirit who is the mutual love of the Father and the Son is the bond of the Trinity, and as their missionary love toward humans is the bond of Creation.[43]

To introduce this subject—the philosophy of Christ—Erasmus cites examples from human philosophy, since he did not view reason and revelation, or creation and redemption, as divided. There are Platonists, Pythagoreans, Academics, Stoics, Cynics, Peripatetics, and Epicureans, communities whose members possessed not only a deep understanding of their teachings but also committed them to memory, fought on their behalf, and even died in their defense. Teachers of ancient philosophic schools addressed the most painful problems of human life, working as compassionate physicians of the soul whose arts could heal many types of human suffering. Their practice of philosophy, the love of wisdom as a way of life, was for the purpose of displaying neither intellectual superiority nor rhetorical cleverness, but was a pastoral activity of grappling with human misery, self-deception, distorted passions and disordered loves; or a "therapy of desire." Philosophers made therapeutic use of speech, utilizing words as instruments of pastoral care—or psychagogy—to promote human happiness through seeking and learning to live wisely and well.[44]

While acknowledging the appropriate role of ancient philosophy in promoting the human good, Erasmus considered it foolish that Christians would ascribe to Aristotle or any other teacher authority equal to that of Christ. Only Christ's wisdom is worthy of our wholehearted desire and pursuit, since it presents a simpler and more satisfying form of life in learning from its Teacher and adhering to its Author.

> He who was a teacher who came forth from heaven, He alone can teach certain doctrine, since it is eternal wisdom, He alone, the sole author of human salvation, taught what pertains to salvation, He alone vouches for whatever he taught, He alone is able to grant whatsoever he has promised.[45]

Christ is the source and goal of the Christian life, just as Christ is the center of theological and pastoral wisdom. Moreover, Christ is the teacher of the Word, the "conversation" of the Father inscribed in the scriptural text and the text of human lives. From the time of the Greek Apologists, adherents of Christianity had absorbed the wisdom of Christ, or *philosophia*, as a way of living. The love of Christian wisdom was exercised through thought, affection, and speech within the ethos and life of Christian communities. Learning to read Scripture cultivated habits of the heart and mind by focusing on its content, form, and dispositions for the enhancement of faith and virtue. Christian philosophy, then, was a way of thinking, desiring, and speaking congruent with the mind of Christ—the true Philosophy himself.[46]

> Christ's law of love always shines before the believer who advances the narrow path of piety, with grace incessantly being present to assist in making progress

toward perfection. Indeed, future happiness already informs Christians' life, but in such a way that they are blessed by hope rather than possession. Cooperating with divine grace, then, human beings bring forth good works which are so evident to other that they glorify God who is in heaven. For it is through the way the Christian walks that God is disgraced or glorified. So, salvation must be pursued by works of love which spring from the root of faith.[47]

Why is Christ's philosophy unique? Erasmus exclaims, "To teach this wisdom God became man; He who was in the heart of the Father descended to earth, rendering foolish the entire wisdom of the world." As the eternal image of God, Christ, the God-Man carries within himself the entire invisible realm. While training in a school of philosophy is not sufficient for attaining full knowledge of Christ, a humble mind and simple faith will do, "The journey is simple, and is ready for anyone." Advancement is granted to those who are receptive and willing; that is, those whom Christ, as a good teacher, inspires and draws, communicating the wisdom of piety to eager minds:[48]

> Erasmus understood faith as a gift of God in Christ which engenders personal trust and commitment. But . . . faith is also a matter of intellectual knowledge and affirmation. Faith is therefore not only a disposition of the heart but a constitution of the mind, and a motivation of the will, for that matter.[49]

Theology is a human participation in the gospel, the conversation of Christ; the human speech of the Father who draws disciples to the circle of true learning within the Triune economy of love.

> For Scripture has been generated by Christ's spirit. Consequently, no one can grasp its essential truth except those who by evangelical faith partake of his spirit . . . one cannot enter the sacred text unless one shares the same spirit. Therefore, without Christ and faith the fountain of canonical Scripture cannot flow. . . . And in the faithful who enters in humility and walks in the spirit of Christ, God's word will bring to fruition what it promises, it will do what it says. The text transforms persons by drawing them into itself.[50]

Erasmus believed that Christ accommodates his wisdom to all who love him and that his embrace will include the highest to the lowest without regard to one's position in life. Since Christ and his wisdom are more common than the sun, only the proud are excluded from his reach. Because the humble and lowly are invited to share in Christ's riches—the Gospels and the Epistles—so too, will "the farmer sing some portion of them at his plow, the weaver hum some parts of them to the movement of his shuttle, the traveler lighten the weariness of the journey with stories of this kind."[51]

The Bible is both the book of Christ and the book of the church; the language of Scripture is the medium through which the life of faith and love is renewed since that the divine *sermo* has come into the world as the expression of God's wisdom and power. Moreover, when word of Christ is translated into life, a person will speak a living language, simply and from the heart, that will instruct, exhort, incite, and encourage others.[52] Emphasizing the study of Scripture, the wisdom of Christ, and the significance of preaching, Erasmus united knowledge, piety, and the language of faith in service of the Spirit. "Language plays a pivotal role in Erasmus' thinking. . . . The truth of both the sensible and intelligible world is so deeply embedded in the word that there is no other way to comprehend it than by reading and hearing, and no other way to communicate it than by writing and speaking."[53]

Many in England heard the *Paraclesis* as a persuasive call to take up a way of reading that would nurture godly learning, living, and speaking. Erasmus rejoiced in the regenerative power of Christ's grace in restoring humanity to its original goodness. While this wisdom is found in nature, it is perfectly proclaimed in Scripture, which is inscribed with power to effect what its Author has spoken. Everything required has been provided: a teacher and model to imitate, divine happiness and satisfaction for the mind, healing for troubled souls, passion and strength for the journey as learners of Christ. Erasmus summoned readers to this journey: "Let us, therefore, with our whole heart covet this literature, let us embrace it, at length let us die in its embrace, let us be transformed in it, since indeed studies are transmuted into morals."[54]

Erasmus' aim was to direct his readers to the words of Scripture since they render "the living image of his [Christ's] holy mind and the speaking, healing, dying, rising Christ Himself. . . so fully present that you would see less if you gazed upon him with your very eyes."[55] For this reason, the *Paraclesis* was a significant work for preachers, demonstrating the life-changing power of faith in Christ who is rendered present by means of the scriptural text, the divine *sermo* spoken by the Father in the persuasiveness of the Spirit. As Hoffman concludes, for Erasmus "Christ is the living word of God, the image of God's mind, and as such he is the supreme preacher endowed with the utmost power of persuasion."[56] Because preaching is learned best from others who have received Christ's wisdom, one should not speak without first being taught by God. However, when Scripture is read with a desire to know and obey, God answers prayer and grants wisdom.

In Christ's school of preaching, reading and listening come before speaking, wisdom before style, and truth before expression. The better and clearer the theology, as taught by Christ, the more persuasive the speech, since a purity of heart allows God to speak more truly and efficaciously.[57] As Wabuda observes, "The person of the preacher was the pivot, in the sacredness of the moment, the mouthpiece of the wisdom of God, infused with the spirit of Christ, who dwelt in his heart."[58] A preacher cannot shine without burning; cannot inflame others without the mind being fired and without the transport of thought. Only when preaching and life, study and prayer, are one, is God's wisdom able to pass into the lives of others through the Spirit's persuasions. Thus a person who aspires to speak God's word must be so consumed and transformed by what and by whom is spoken that he or she becomes a living instrument of Christ.[59]

> For Erasmus language is the fundamental signature of all reality. . . . This is preeminently true for theology, that all encompassing word of salvation, the message of ultimate wholeness. So from God the fountain proceeds Christ the word and image of God. But Christ is present for us in sacred Scripture, the medium that actually now embodies the divine mediator between God and humankind. For this reason the Scripture represents the heavenly origin from which the word of proclamation has to take its beginning. The biblical canon constitutes the objective primary source of preaching.[60]

The wisdom of the *Novum Testamentum* was supplemented by the publication of the *Paraphrases on the New Testament* (1517–24) that provided preachers with a continuous exposition of Scripture that renders the wisdom of Christ in homiletic form.[61] As Cardinal Campeggi wrote to Erasmus in 1519,

"I seized every opportunity to acquire your image, which I found reflected . . . most recently in your sermon-paraphrase on the Pauline Epistles."[62] His sermon-paraphrase "says things differently without saying different things, especially in a subject which is not only difficult, but sacred, and very near the majesty of the Gospel."[63] Mark Vessey describes this work:

> As a series of evangelical orations, Erasmus' Paraphrases . . . are a natural embod-
> iment of their author's intent to make the Word of God effective in his own age:
> only if the gospel were heard again in its most persuasive form, the humanist
> rhetorician believed, could it move human beings to the life of Christ—like
> piety in which their salvation lay. . . . Virtual scripts for preaching rather than
> transcripts of sermons actually preached, they are the work of a man who was
> making the printing press his pulpit and who would always rely on others to give
> physical voice to the gospel message as he phrased it.[64]

The aim of the sermon-paraphrases was to render the meaning of the Bible by offering more than translation but less than commentary, communicating *by means* of the language of Scripture rather than *about* the language of Scripture. In other words, the aim of the *Paraphrases* was to get the mind of Christ off the pages of Scripture and into the minds of readers, since Christ is the content, goal, and final efficient cause of spiritual regeneration and moral transformation.[65] If used wisely, the words of Scripture and the words of the *Paraphrases* would serve a mediating function, respectively, between Christ and the church, Erasmus and readers, preachers and people.[66]

The evangelical piety of Erasmus was a moving force for theological, spiritual, and moral renewal in sixteenth- and seventeenth-century England.[67] His work helped to pave the way for others to prove what Scripture could achieve by cul-tivating the wisdom engendered by Christ as God's human speech.[68] Interpreting both the biblical text and contemporary context, Erasmus presented himself as a model of practical wisdom through the expression of scriptural discourse.[69] In his *Paraphrase on 1 Peter 4*, Erasmus describes how this spiritual transformation serves the word of Christ in both preaching and hearing.

> If it falls to a person's lot to receive sacred doctrine or the gift of a learned
> tongue, he is not to use it for personal gain or pride or empty glory but for the
> salvation of his neighbor and the glory of Christ, and his audience should

perceive that the words they hear are from God, not from men, and that the one who speaks to them is but an instrument of the divine voice.[70]

The business of preaching is to offer Christ, the eloquent "sermon" of God who communicates himself through the words and actions of pastors who have been transformed by the Word in Scripture through the work of the Spirit.[71] Wabadu writes:

> The preacher must be the first to permit his heart to be transformed. . . . The preacher's potency came from responding to the call of God, to the ecstatic vision of love, of being swept away and ravished. His new heart and rectitude were hidden, by the folds of scripture, inside his very being, his old heart exchanged for God's. Transmuted and infused, his was not the wisdom of the world, but the sublimity of God lent to him, and it was the deep reliance upon divine action, expressed through the Holy Spirit, which was central to Erasmus' portrait of any devout Christian, but the particular treasure of the preacher. In the hushed expectancy of the assembly, the coming together of the members of Christ, as the holy company of heaven drew near to listen and partake together with the living, the sermon represented the mystical meeting place between the earthly and divine, the charismatic moment for the imparting of sacred wisdom, an aural revelation of the truth of God, made possible by the action of the Holy Spirit upon the speaker, and upon those in attendance, so that understanding flowed into the hearts and minds of the listeners.[72]

The practical wisdom of Erasmus had a formative influence in uniting learning, piety, and ministry within the Anglican tradition.[73] Trumpeting the transformative power of Scripture as transcending external forms of religion, and promoting the inward apprehension of trust in divine grace that bears fruit in good works, Erasmus summoned readers to participate in the renewal of Christian faith and love. His program called for reform of neither ideas nor social structures, but pressed instead for more radical shifts in understanding and desire to promote the spiritual and moral renewal of the church; especially among its pastoral leaders. According to Erasmus, the pastoral vocation entails a transformation to evangelical godliness that rests on sincere faith and true love—for God, the self, and others—habits of thought, devotion, and speech he hoped would overcome divisions between Christ, the Word of Scripture, and the ministry of preaching.

Wesley and "Learned Piety"

In a manner similar to the practical wisdom of Erasmus, John Wesley's *An Address to the Clergy* turns attention to the character of pastoral ministry, describing the kind of exemplary wisdom and virtue that serves as fitting instruments of the truth and goodness mediated by God's Wisdom incarnated by Christ. As did Erasmus, Wesley integrates theology and life, uniting knowledge and love in counseling pastors that the work of ministry has its basis in, and springs from, devotion of the heart and mind to God.

> What is a Minister of Christ, a shepherd of souls, unless he is devoted to God? Unless he abstain, with the utmost care and diligence, from every evil word and work; from all appearance of evil; yea, from the most innocent things, whereby any might be offended or made weak? Is he not called, above others, to be an example to the flock, in his private as well as public character; an example of all holy and heavenly tempers, filling the heart so as to shine through the life? . . . Do I understand my own office? Have I deeply considered before God the character which I bear? What is it to be an Ambassador of Christ, and Envoy from the King of heaven? And do I know and feel what is implied in "watching over the souls' of men 'as he that must give an account?"[74]

Appropriating the knowledge of Scripture into pastoral ministry requires and leads to practical wisdom, the expression of "doctrine coming to life" in the declaration of living faith. Such "knowledge in action" is dependent upon the presence of the Holy Spirit whose illuminating work cleanses the eyes of the heart and understanding to "see" connections between God's Word in Scripture and God's work in the lives of people.

> Consequently, is not his whole life, if he walks worthy of his calling, one incessant labour of love; one continued tract of praising God, and helping man; one series of thankfulness and beneficence? Is he not always humble, always serious, though rejoicing evermore; mild, gentle, patient, and abstinent? . . . Is he not one sent forth from God, to stand between God and man, to guard and assist the poor, helpless children of men, to supply them both with light and strength to guide them through a thousand known and unknown dangers, till at the

appointed time he returns, with those committed to his charge, to his and their Father who is in heaven?[75]

Like Erasmus, Wesley encouraged pastors to immerse themselves in prayerful study of Scripture to receive its saving wisdom and to speak its truth in love. This way of reading nurtures both the knowledge of God and human excellence; the formation of a certain kind of person endued with the wisdom of love—to God and the neighbor in God—that enables judgment for seeing God's work within the particular circumstances of life.

> Am I, . . . such as I ought to be, with regard to my affections? I am taken from among, and ordained for, men, in things pertaining to God. I stand between God and man, by the authority of the great Mediator, in the nearest and most endearing relation both to my Creator and to my fellow creatures. Have I accordingly given my heart to God, and to my brethren for his sake? And my neighbor, every man, as myself? Does this love swallow me up, possess me whole, all my passions and tempers, and regulate all my faculties and powers? Is it the spring which gives rise to all my thoughts, and governs all my words and actions?[76]

Articulating a spiritually rich understanding of pastoral ministry, Wesley affirmed the union of learning and piety that illumines the mind in nurturing personal acquaintance with the "treasuries of sacred knowledge." By following the way of holiness, the affections of the heart and mind are purified and reoriented to God, a transformation that radiates through one's thoughts, words, and actions, or "conversation." The study of Scripture induces love for God and knowledge of God's saving wisdom in Christ—the end internal to all aspects related to the practice of preaching and ministry.

> Ought not a "steward of the mysteries of God," a shepherd of the souls for whom Christ died, to be endued with an eminent measure of love to God and love to all his brethren? a love the same in kind, but in degree far beyond that of ordinary Christians? Can he otherwise answer the high character he bears, and the relation wherein he stands? Without this, how can he go through all the toils and difficulties which neccesarily attend the faithful execution of his office? Would it be possible for a parent to go through the pain and fatigue of bearing and bringing up children were it not for that vehement affection, storge [natural affection] which the Creator has given for that very end? How much less will it

be possible for any Pastor, any spiritual parent, to go through the pain and labor of "travailing in birth for," and bringing up, many children to the measure of the full stature of Christ, without a large measure of that inexpressible affection which "a stranger intermeddleth not with"![77]

Wesley's understanding of pastoral ministry is situated within the Anglican tradition of faith working through love, a heritage of practical divinity, which in large part traces its roots to the Christian humanism of Erasmus that unites intellectual and moral virtue in piety or devotion to God. Seen from this perspective, preaching is best understood as the expression of "truth in action"—an integrated way of thinking, living, and speaking that is engendered by grace and participates in the knowledge and love of Christ. The truth of God matters in preaching.

BACK TO THE FUTURE

N earing the end of his life, John Wesley looked across almost sixty years of ministry and described the practical wisdom of Methodism as an eighteenth-century expression of the Pentecostal pattern in Acts 2 and 4. His remembrance invoked a vision of shared life that was thoroughly committed to Christian orthodoxy, not only to the three ancient creeds but also to the teaching of the Church of England as contained in its *Articles of Religion* and *Book of Homilies*.

> They were all precisely of one judgment as well as of one soul. All tenacious of order to the last degree, and observant, for conscience' sake, of every rule of the church. . . . They were all orthodox in every point; firmly believing not only the three creeds, but whatsoever they judged to be the doctrine of the Church of England, as contained in her Articles and Homilies. As to that practice of the apostolic church (which continued till the time of Tertullian, at least in many churches) the "having all things in common," they had no rule, nor any formed design concerning it. But it was so, in effect, and it could not be otherwise; for none could want anything that another could not spare.[1]

Wesley insisted the faith of "Methodists" was the true religion of the Bible as developed by the Church of England and "traditioned" through its *Book of Common Prayer, Articles of Religion,* and official *Homilies,* documents that served to fill the hearts and minds of people with the knowledge and love of God. On numerous occasions, Wesley expressed this commitment, writing of the common life he shared with others according to the principles of the Church of England as confirmed by its liturgy, articles, and homilies, and by the whole tenor of Scripture.[2]

As a homiletic theologian, Wesley's life and vocation was defined by the gospel: "I indeed live by preaching."[3] As a preacher and teacher of preachers, his homiletic wisdom was nourished by the teaching of Scripture with the guidance of the official *Books of Homilies* published under Edward VI and Elizabeth I; formularies to which Wesley was ever eager to confess his allegiance. During the latter years of his ministry, upon returning from a tour of Methodist societies throughout England and Ireland, Wesley reported:

> The book, which next to the Holy Scriptures was of greatest use to them in settling their judgment as to the grand point of justification by faith, is the book of Homilies. They were never clearly convinced that we are justified by faith alone till they carefully consulted these and compared them with the sacred writings [Holy Scripture]. And no minister of the Church can, with any decency, oppose these, seeing that at his ordination he subscribed to them in subscribing to the thirty-sixth article of the Church.[4]

Almost fifty years earlier, Wesley had provided a doctrinal summary for Methodist preaching by printing an extract of the *Doctrine of Salvation, Faith and Good Works* from the *Homilies of the Church of England*.[5] This tract defined a position from which he never wavered: living faith in Christ that works through loving devotion and grateful obedience to God. He writes, "I began more narrowly to inquire what the doctrine of the Church of England is concerning the much-controverted point of justification by faith; and the sum of what I found in the homilies, I extracted and printed for the use of others."[6]

The purpose of the official homilies was to direct readers, especially preachers, to diligent study of Scripture with assurance that God acts through the Holy Spirit to grant living faith in Christ that is energized by love.[7] For Wesley, the road to the future led through the past. By turning "back to the future" he discovered in the soteriology and homiletic wisdom of the Church of England a "grammar" for Methodist preaching, evangelization, and catechesis. Moreover, while the Bible was the chief source of the homilies, the liturgical ethos of Anglicanism was their home. Summoned by the truth and goodness of God revealed in the Gospels, gatherings of prayer, praise, and proclamation were occasions for grateful response to the astonishing overflow of the Father's pure, unbounded love in the ministry of the Son through the power of the Spirit; a trinitarian vision of salvation that constituted and was expressed by the evangelical and sacramental character of Methodism.[8]

It may be that Wesley's Anglican turn "back to the future" is not typically remembered in relation to either his "heart warming" conversion at Aldersgate or his subsequent decision to take up field preaching; significant events that are often interpreted as the result of self-directed experience and pragmatic judgment. However, what is often overlooked is Wesley's discovery that true faith is directed outward to the work God has done in Jesus Christ for the salvation of the world, the result of a profound intellectual and spiritual orientation that was illumined by Scripture and confirmed by the theological wisdom of the church's official homilies.

William Abraham challenges the standard account of Wesley's "background music," which tends to place him within an emerging modern world, liberated from ecclesial tradition and authority, while guided by self-enlightenment in pursuing a life of reason, freedom, experience, tolerance, individual opinion, and evidence provided by scientific discovery. Set against this background, Wesley is often interpreted in the following manner:

> He is the great exponent of personal religion, staying the course until he finds God for himself at the famous Aldersgate meeting. He is the mighty champion of creative innovation, breaking from the shackles of his Anglican tradition to reach out to those who are trampled aside by established religion. While he reads voraciously and is fascinated by past history, he thinks for hmself, writing in clear prose and with self-confidence. Whenever there is a choice between the demands of the poor and marginalized, he always takes sides with the latter, taking on big battalions of business and vested interests. At heart he is a man of reason and experience, thus lining up with John Locke in philosophy and finding a way to express the Christian faith in a manner that is up to speed with the latest in the world of learning. While he is a traditionalist in his leanings in worship, he recognizes that fashions change, and that it is, therefore, urgent to make innovations in worship and evangelism. He is a whirlwind of energy, organizing self-help programs that meet the needs of the hour and providing structures that foster naïve leadership and cross generational efficiency.[9]

Abraham concludes that when Wesley's ministry and theology are abstracted from the confessional and sacramental framework of trinitarian and incarnational faith, what is left is a hopelessly reduced vision of Christian faith and life. Albert Outler similarly observed that a forgetfulness of Wesley's theological convictions inevitably leads to "pious sentimentality," "narcissism," and "emotive anti-intellectualism," and alternatively, an "overconfidence in reason," which is bolstered by a variety of empiricisms, abstractions, and pragmatic appeals for achieving "practical results."[10]

It may be that those who hold to the "standard account" described by Abraham have either forgotten or chosen to ignore Wesley's lifelong commitment to the Church of England and its common life of doctrine, liturgy, and discipline. Jason Vickers argues convincingly that Wesley was a "representative Anglican"—a particular ecclesial loyalty and correlative way of life that requires attention if we are to arrive at a clearer understanding of Wesley's homiletic theology and practice of preaching. As Vickers comments on interpretations of Wesley that tend to follow the standard account:

> Taken together, scholarly judgments that Wesley's actions undermined his words and that the Church of England in the eighteenth century was lax, corrupt and spiritually compromised serve to reinforce the popular image of Wesley as a rebel in thought as well as action. Surely we are dealing here with someone who, recognizing that the church was corrupt to the core, did whatever it took to help people come to know and love God, a virtual one man evangelistic enterprise. Surely Wesley's life and ministry reflect how bad things really were in the established church. Surely by the end of his life, if not well before, he was dreaming of starting his own church.[11]

Vickers suggests that the standard reading of Wesley makes for great "sound bytes" in support of two dominant views: (1) that Wesley was either an eighteenth-century conservative reactionary who resisted the increase of secularization in England, acting in pragmatic ways and doing anything that would reach people; and (2) that Wesley was a protomodernist and progressive who was willing to "work outside the box" to lead a settled old church, stuck in its traditional ways of thinking, into a brave new world of human enlightenment. In either interpretation, Wesley is seen as a reactionary against the Church of England, a rebellious clergyman whose strategy was oriented either backward or forward in time, and one whose perceived strength, as an evangelist or agent of social change, was dependent upon the weakness, decline, and stubborn resistance of the established church.[12]

Stephen Long's work shows that many interpretations of Wesley assume a modern, logical-positivist framework of reality and then fit his work within it. What this means, however, is that Wesley ends up being viewed as an empirical, pragmatic thinker who reduces things to technical method rather than seeing them in light of their fundamental orientation to God. A consequence of this view is that doctrine, liturgy, sacraments, and the discipline of the church are no longer necessary or relevant to understand, let alone appreciate, Wesley's theological and pastoral wisdom. Long writes:

> Methodist and Wesleyan theologians tended to embrace the modern epoch. It offered promise to the Wesleyan Christian tradition, for which forms of Christianity that were wedded to outmoded forms of thought (Catholicism, Anglicanism, Orthodoxy). Methodism has an adaptability to it that positioned it well to be relevant to the modern era. Then came the end of modernity, and what was once Methodism's promise has become the limitation. The modern Wesley who can always be made relevant for today—either conservative or liberal—now prevents this brand of the Christian ecumene from discerning the present times and speaking a theological word in them.[13]

Freed from his creedal, sacramental, and ecclesial commitments, Wesley is pressed into the service of pragmatic and revisionist agendas. On the one hand, his work is seen as useful and applicable for achieving success measured by pragmatic goals; on the other, his work can be made relevant to fit current intellectual trends and fashions.

Here it is interesting to consider the current emphasis on secularization in North America. Bryan Stone's analysis of this position shows how the predominate strategy for convincing presumably "secular" people of the truth of Christianity has been to demonstrate its relevance on terms agreeable to their understanding or to market its usefulness for addressing their deeply felt concerns and needs. In other words, the factuality and utility of Christianity is set forth by appealing to foundations external—rather than internal—to the content and truth of Christian doctrine as grounded in the gospel of Jesus Christ. Stone describes these contemporary ways of appropriating Christianity for evangelism that bear similarities to the standard account of Wesley's ministry.

The first is preoccupied with establishing the intellectual respectability of the gospel in terms of purportedly wider or more universal criteria for what counts as truth and plausibility. The second busies itself with demonstrating the practical value and usefulness of Christian faith for persons in a society that determines value by the logic of the marketplace and measures usefulness by service to the nation, the economy, or the private well being of individual egos.[14]

Challenging the standard account of Wesley—as either a conservative reactionary or liberal protomodernist—Vickers argues that Wesley was and remained a representative Anglican who admonished Methodists to adhere closely to the doctrine of the Church of England and to participate in its sacramental life as often as possible. To this end, Wesley even provided revised editions of the *Thirty Nine Articles of Religion* and the *Book of Common Prayer* for American Methodists; the former to ensure belief in the Trinity, the latter frequent reception of the sacraments.[15]

My particular interest in this chapter focuses on Wesley's turn to the *Book of Homilies*; their contribution to shaping his understanding of living faith that works through love, and their importance for his homiletic theology and practice. Albert Outler calls attention to the significance of this Anglican turn in the aftermath of Wesley's heart-warming experience of God's assurance at Aldersgate in 1738.[16] This dawning discovery is described in Wesley's Journal for May 24, 1738, which reports on his exchanges with the Moravians.

> When I met Peter Bohler again, he readily consented to put the dispute upon the issue which I desired, viz., Scripture and experience. I first consulted the Scripture. But when I set aside the glosses of men, and simply considered the words of God . . . I found they all made against me, and was forced to retreat to my last hold, "that experience would never agree with the literal interpretation of those Scriptures. Nor could I therefore allow it to be true, till I found some living experiences of it." He replied, he could show me such at any time. . . . And accordingly the next day he came with three others, all of whom testifed of their own personal experience that true, living faith in Christ is inseparable for a sense of pardon from all past, and freedom from all present sins. They added with one mouth that this faith was the gift, the free gift of God, and that he would surely bestow it upon every soul who earnestly and perseveringly sought it. I was now thoroughly convinced.[17]

Outler considers Wesley's abridgment of the first four homilies authorized in 1547 during the reign of Edward VI—*The Doctrine of Salvation, Faith, and Good Works, Extracted from the Homilies of the Church of England*—to be a "theological manifesto." The result is a union of soteriology and ethics, or doctrine and life that gives strong affirmation to the primacy of faith in Christ that is energized by love and nourished by good works. In other words, the end of faith is righteousness, living faith working through love for God and the neighbor; a life happy in accord with God's design and holy in accord with God's desire. A look at the nature and purpose of the homilies will be helpful for understanding the significance of Wesley's turn back to their doctrinal wisdom to find his way forward.

English Reformation scholarship has tended to underestimate the dramatically subversive and reconstructive potential of sixteenth-century reforming discourse and its antecedent reformist traditions. In England, as on the Continent, preaching for the reform of Christian faith and life proved central, continuing, and expanding a trend that emerged in the fourteenth and fifteenth centuries, and that took a dramatic leap during the Henrician period under the direction of Thomas Cromwell and Thomas Cranmer. Reformers exploited sermons effectively, taking over the mendicant tradition of publicly attacking the corruption of church and society. They utilized the pulpit to teach new doctrine, to introduce new practices, to articulate new visions, and to move their listeners to embrace them through the preaching of the Word of God.[18]

A significant example of the Edwardian's confidence in the efficacy of preaching was the assembling of the first *Book of Homilies*, which was issued in 1547 to both communicate and control the central convictions of the reform, defining a vision of evangelical faith and life for the transformation of the realm into a Christian commonwealth under the Royal Supremacy of Edward VI.[19] Changes in religious ideas, practices, language and identity that were begun or achieved during Edward's reign were in no small part due to the work of preachers and their homiletic or "preached" theology. Claiming Scripture as both their authority and model, these reformist preachers were, in the words of Patrick Collinson, "living in the pages of the Bible."[20]

John Wall argues that the English Reformation was driven in large part by the printing, distribution, and use of religious books as instruments of religious and institutional reform, as vehicles for the dissemination of Edwardian policies and intentions for the spiritual welfare of the people.[21] The story of the English Reformation may therefore be seen from the perspective provided by its great books: *The English Bible*, the *Book of Homilies*, Erasmus' *Paraphrases of the New Testament*, and the *Book of Common Prayer*.[22] The *Royal Injunctions* promulgated in July 1547 required every parish church in England to have the "whole Bible, of the largest volume in Englishe," Erasmus' *Paraphrases on the Gospels and Acts*, and a collection of twelve sermons, known as the *Book of Homilies*, for use in reading, Bible study, and preaching. By making the Scriptures available in the language of the people, Thomas Cranmer intended to construct a renewed English church built upon a theology of the Word, believing that biblical speech, properly presented in its various forms, contains the power to engage and transform the world in which it is spoken, heard, and obeyed.[23]

The *Book of Homilies* represents Cranmer's ambition to issue a collection of sermons to remedy the shortage of reliable preachers in the church. This culminated in a plan under Edward that was begun during the reign of Henry VIII, having predecessors in the various occasional addresses issued by Cromwell, the format of the *Ten Articles*, and the 1537 *Bishops' Book*, which provided insufficiently trained priests with a doctrinal summary and a framework for biblical interpretation and sermon construction. Cranmer's concern in the homilies was to establish the nature of salvation as God's free gift of faith, while demonstrating to both preachers and persons in the pew that this affirmation did not represent a collapse of morality; that good works still formed an essential part of the Christian life. Yet the homilies also represent a significant shift in theological emphasis, since a whole range of traditional practices were eliminated and the range of works was redefined and narrowed.[24]

While they resembled medieval homilaries, books of model sermons on which untrained parish priests could rely when discharging the duty of regular preaching, the Edwardian homilies also introduced an economy of salvation in which sermons played the central part; a homiletic theology. This established them as significant agents of religious renewal and reform, instruments for promoting faith, love and obedience to God that derived their authority from two sources, a preface issued in the name of the king, and the thirty-second injunction that anticipated significant coming religious changes.

> Because through lack of preachers in many places of the King's realms and dominions the people continue in ignorance and blindness, all persons, vicars, and curates shall read in their churches every Sunday one of the homilies, which are and shall be set forth for the same purpose by the king's authority, in such sort as the shall be appointed to do in the preface of the same.[25]

This injunction made reading the homilies for all but the few licensed preachers of the realm a binding responsibility. However, the *Book of Homilies* was published not only to assist nonpreaching prelates but also to serve as an instructing and regulating homiletic guide for learned preachers. The homilies thus provided a grammar of evangelical doctrine and life; a practically ordered, theological framework according to essential topics derived from Scripture for ensuring doctrinal consistency across the realm.[26]

This was of particular importance during a time of confusion and change, when conservative priests were resistant to Protestant reforms, and when the more tolerant atmosphere of Edward's reign encouraged an increase of maverick preachers, or "gospellers."[27] "*Certayne Sermons or Homilies, appoynted by the Kinges Majestie, to be declared and redde, by all persones (parsons) Vicars, Curates, every Sundaye in their Churches, where they have Cure*" were published to address these challenges, demonstrating Cranmer's desire that there be weekly pastoral instruction for the transformation of parishioners' lives by means of Scripture's language and wisdom being spoken in the vernacular.

The homilies were initially experienced through the ear, not the eye, and with the authorization of the *Book of Common Prayer* in 1549, they provided regular opportunities for English people to be incorporated into Scripture's drama of salvation, the most vital impulse for refashioning both church and nation.[28] Nicholas Ridley acknowledged the practical aim of the homilies was in keeping with medieval precedence, asserting that some were "in commendation of the principal virtues that are commended in scripture," and "others against the most pernicious and capital vices that useth (alas!) to reign in this realm of England."[29]

As a form of preached theology, the practical wisdom of the homilies was well suited for large diverse groups of listeners. As John King points out, homily, "conversation, or instruction," corresponds to sermon, *sermo*, or "word," but ultimately derives from "crowd, or mob," reflecting the outdoor circumstances under which Jesus, Paul, and the apostles preached. By analogy with the Incarnation, the plain style of the homilies paradoxically unites the highest and the lowest, the heavenly and the earthly, in a plain, modest style that corresponds to its subject matter; revelation, instruction, and persuasion for Christians living in the world. King argues that the world of Edwardian England that was addressed by the homilies was a diverse world. Its complexity paralleled that of the Elizabethan stage; reflecting the "high and low" composition of audiences envisioned by Cranmer in compiling the homilies, and the "high to low" movement of the Word through the learned but humble preaching exemplified by the language and style of the homilies.[30]

Wall concludes the *Book of Homilies* calls for Christian action nourished by faith that works through love and leads to eternal life. In this important matter the homilies follow the biblical vision conveyed in the writings of Erasmus, enlarging its framework to include society as a whole. It is both a religious and political document, representing a move toward greater reform in the church and greater consolidation of authority for its enactment in the hands of a godly prince. The scope of the homilies is therefore defined in the preface in terms of moving the people "to honor and worship almighty God, and diligently to serve hym." This means serving the king "with all humilitie and subjeccion," . . . "godly and honestly, behaving themselves toward all men." Modeled after Erasmus' philosophy of Christ, the character of this reform was based on a humanist vision of the imitation of Christ, consisting of a life of faith and active charity in all aspects of English society.[31]

Because the Bible was the primary source for the homilies their aim was to imitate the language of Scripture, in particular, its images, figures, and examples.[32] This biblically derived style renders the sermons more forceful and vivid, increases their clarity and immediacy, while at the same time rooting their content in the soil of Scripture. In addition, the homilies offer persuasive models for imitation in the life of discipleship, since a devout Christian people was the truest demonstration of living faith. This life is depicted throughout the ordering of the homilies; listeners are first called to a knowledge of Scripture and then to God's acts of redemption that evoke living faith as the means to love that is the end of God's commandments.[33]

The first homily communicates this overarching purpose, making clear the book is Bible centered and draws its inspiration, scope, and style from Scripture, "the heavenly meate of our soules." Through reading and hearing Scripture—devouring and absorbing its message—Christians are transformed into the Word they digest and thus energized to do what it says for attaining the gift of salvation: "The words of holy scripture . . . have power to convert through God's promise, and to be effectuall, through God's assistance."[34] The aim of the homilies was to transfigure the lives of listeners by enfolding them into the saving wisdom of Scripture through consistent, disciplined reading and hearing in the worshiping life of the church.[35]

Wesley's Homiletic Theology

Robert Cushman notes that Wesley's "practical divinity" was the fruit of his received emendation of the doctrine of the Church of England as found in the homilies.[36] There Wesley discovered the difference between historical faith and saving faith; not only faith that assents outwardly, but also faith that is living, a "sure trust and confidence in the mercy of God through Jesus Christ." In other words, to believe that the Bible speaks infallibly, to affirm the content of the creed, and to give assent to the Articles of Religion, is not the faith that saves, a distinction that was clarified for Wesley in the homily "Of Salvation." There he learned that confession is not a general proposition or principle, but is a confession grounded upon faith in God, just as confession praises and gives thanks to God for the work of Jesus Christ. As the homily states:

> But that this true doctrine of justification by faith may be truly understood, [observe that] justification is the office of God only and is not a thing which we render unto him but which we receive of him by his free mercy, thouth the only merits of his beloved Son. . . . The right and true Christian faith is not only to believe that Holy Scripture and the articles of faith are true, but also to have a

sure trust and confidence to be saved from everlasting damnation by Christ, whereof doth follow a loving heart to obey his commandments.[37]

True and living faith is not only an act of understanding but also a disposition of the heart, a sure trust and confidence toward the work of God in Christ. In other words, when faith is true it will receive a loving disposition in the heart toward God. This love is both inward and external; love that is intelligent, passionate, and practical, fulfilling the law as the end of God's commandment.

The homily, "Of the Christian Faith" further defines living faith as active and working, as the necessary means that is in order to the love and goodness that constitute human flourishing:

> This is the true, living Christian faith [which] is not in the mouth and outward profession only, but it liveth and stirreth inwardly in the heart. And this faith is not without hope and trust in God nor without the love of God and of our neighbor, nor without the fear of God, nor without the desire to hear God's Word and follow the same in [avoiding] evil and gladly doing all good works.[38]

The homily goes on to give more explicit definition to the virtues and good works that spring from living faith that works through love for God and neighbor; a life of discipline that actively seeks and promotes the good declared by the law.

> [Let us then by our works declare] our faith to be the [living] Christian faith, and by such virtues as ought to spring out of faith, "let us add to (or in) [our] faith, virtue, knowledge; in [our] knowledge, termperance; in (our) temperance, patience; in (our) patience, godliness, in our] godliness, brotherly [kindness]; and in brotherly [kindness], charity" [cf. 2 Pet. 1:9]. So shall we both certify our conscience [that we are in the right fatih] and also confirm other men. If you feel and perceive such a faith in you, rejoice in it and be diligent to maintain it. Let it be daily increasing more and more by [good works]. So shall you be sure that you shall please God, when his will is, "receive the end of your faith, [even] the salvation of your souls" (1 Pet. 1:9).[39]

For Wesley, a life that consists of wisdom and virtue is grounded in the gift of faith and the effectual work of the Spirit. In other words, good works without the life of faith is dead. On the other hand, if faith is true it will receive the gift of hope, which desires the good God promises, and the gift of love, which obeys the law of love as the end of God's dispensations and works. Faith is the means to holiness while love is its end. The way into sanctification is a "participation in the divine nature, a putting on of the mind that was in Christ, and the renewal of the heart after the image of God."[40] We therefore come to God through God, rather than by our own ingenuity and efforts—trusting the merits of Christ and the power of the Holy Spirit—as conveyed through the witness of Scripture.

For theological reasons, Wesley could refer to Scripture as the "oracles of God" in relation to the proclamation of faith that is engendered by divine illumination and persuasion. Scripture testifies of itself and its authority for all who receive its promises and cease to rely upon their own sufficiency, submitting in penitence of heart to the saving, nurturing and regenerative infusion of God's prevenient grace. Justification by grace through faith—the forgiveness of sins, reconciliation to God, and a new life centered on God, becomes for the receptive hearer the "Scripture way of salvation," which is the wisdom of God. Through the Spirit's illuminating and converting work, the knowledge of faith is made evident by the transformation of mind and heart in conformance to the likeness of Christ.[41]

The homilies had a profound influence on Wesley in his coming to understand that living faith is declared through the proclamation of practical divinity, a knowledgable account of God's coming in Christ through the power of the Spirit to provide a way for humanity to return to God. The spirit and substance of the gospel is conveyed by the preaching of the Word, which in turn supplies doctrinal norms for the practical task of teaching, correcting, defending, and directing the church into the fullness of salvation—in this present life.[42] This unity of theology and practice is reflected by Wesley's comments in the preface to the *Sermons on Several Occasions*:

> I have . . . set down in the following sermons what I find in the Bible concerning the way to heaven, with a vew to distinguishing this way of God from those which are the inventions of men. I have endeavored to describe the true, the scriptural, experimental religion, so as to omit nothing which is a real part

thereof, and to add nothing thereto which is not. And herein it is more especially my desire, first, to guard those who are just setting their faces toward heaven (and, who, having little acquaintance with the things of God, are the more liable to be turned out of the way) from formality, from mere outside religion which has almost driven heart religion out of the world; and secondly, to warn those who know the religion of the heart, "the faith which worketh by love," lest any time they make void of the law through faith and so fall back into the snare of the devil.[43]

By publishing model sermons, Wesley hoped to provide homiletic wisdom oriented to the induction of faith and end of knowing, loving, and enjoying God through the witness of Scripture. It is important to remember that the Anglican tradition, in particular its *Book of Homilies*, turned Wesley back to the teaching of Scripture which, in turn, pointed him to God's work in Christ and the promise of divine empowerment for a life of holiness.

In considering Wesley's practical wisdom, what also deserves our attention is the manner in which saving faith and holiness of life—the content and form of the gospel—gave shape to the witness of the gospel in the activity of preaching, or the "preaching life." It will be helpful to look at Wesley's sermon, "The Means of Grace," which was written not too many years after Aldersgate and his turn back to the official homilies. The sermon shows that Wesley's theological convictions regarding living faith presuppose and inform his practical wisdom regarding the use of Scripture as a means of coming to know and love God.

Wesley's text for the sermon is Malachi 3:7, "Ye are gone away from mine ordinances, and have not kept them."[44] He begins by establishing that ordinances were brought to light by the gospel dispensation in Christ and ordained by God as channels of grace. He turns to Acts 2 to discern this pattern: "all that believed were together, and had all things in common; they continued steadfastly in the teaching of the apostles, and the breaking of bread, and in prayers." He then describes what tends to occur over time; that some will mistake the means for the end, placing external works over a heart renewed after God's image, thereby forgetting that the end of every command is love for God and neighbor. Others will neglect outward means, presuming there is something within themselves that is pleasing to God. Wesley concludes that neither of these approaches is able to conduce the end for which the means of grace have been ordained, the knowledge and love of God.[45] Stephen Long writes:

> There is interplay between the internal and external where we must do certain externals such as assent to creedal Christianity, observe the General Rules, and attend the sacraments. But this doing is never an end. It is a means of waiting on the gift of the Beatitudes and Spirit—infused virtues, which order our lives to God. These gifts only come as we know God in Jesus Christ, as we walk by faith and not by sight. . . . The simplest meaning of faith for Wesley is "assent to knowledge." But that is nothing but a bare external if it does not issue forth in a holy life of joyful obedience, loving God and neighbor. The external presupposes the internal, but the internal cannot be had without the external.[46]

The means of grace are thus understood as outward signs or actions ordained of God and appointed for this end; as ordinary channels that convey prevenient, justifying, and sanctifying grace. After naming prayer, Wesley moves to discuss searching the Scriptures that consists of reading, hearing, and mediating. This is followed by his treatment of the Lord's Supper. What is significant is the manner whereby Wesley grounds these ecclesial practices in the merit of Christ and the power of the Spirit; that is, in living faith, a "trust and confidence" in God as affirmed by the *Book of Homilies*. In other words, there is no intrinsic power in the means other than the power of God, the giver of every good gift and the author of grace. Apart from the Incarnation and Holy Spirit, we cannot attain to the knowledge and love of God that is mediated by Scripture to those who await God's self-giving. Moreover, the means of grace are themselves incapable of accomplishing salvation; they are necessary but not sufficient, since they possess no merit in themselves apart from the completed work of Christ and the efficacy of the Spirit. In other words, Christ is the only means of grace.[47] He is the meritorious cause and the Holy Spirit is the efficient cause of divine grace that grants justification and leads to the fullness of sanctification.

To practice otherwise is to have the form of godliness without its power. If the work of Christ and the efficacy of the Spirit are absent from the reading of Scripture there is neither merit nor virtue in its use. For this reason, Wesley grounds the ordinances and common life of the church in living faith that actively waits for God's presence and gifts. The work of ministry, by which the church is constituted and constitutes itself, is grounded in the merit of Christ through living faith that participates in the economy of salvation through the grace and power of the Spirit. Wesley writes:

> So little do they understand that great foundation of the whole Christian build-
> ing, "By grace ye are saved." Ye are saved from your sins, for the guilt and power
> thereof, ye are restored to the favour and image of God, not for any works, mer-
> its, or deservings of yours, but by the free grace, the mere mercy of God through
> the merits of his well beloved Son. Ye are thus saved, not by any power, wisdom,
> or strength which is in you or in any other creature, but merely through the
> grace and power of the Holy Ghost, which worketh all in all.[48]

Wesley also anticipated the kind of questions this teaching would likely invoke:

> But the main question remains. We know this salvation is the gift and the work
> of God. But how (may one say, who is convinced he hath it not) may I attain
> thereto? If you say, "Believe, and thou shalt be saved," he answers, "True; but
> how shall I believe?" You reply, "Wait upon God." "Well. But how am I to wait?
> In the means of grace, or out of them? Am I to wait for the grace of God which
> bringeth salvation by using these means, or by laying them aside?"[49]

Wesley responds to these questions in his treatment of "searching the Scriptures," defining this as waiting upon God's grace in hearing, reading, and meditating. He offers neither a theory nor an explanation, but asserts that answers to such questions will be found in the practice itself, in the means by which God gives, confirms, and increases knowledge of the true and godly wisdom that constitutes salvation. Seen in this light, the practically wise use of Scripture is profitable for "doctrine, reproof, for correction, for instruction in righteousness, to the end of perfection and all good works."[50] This is a good for those who know God and those who do not, since the brightness of God's glory shines through the prophetic voice of Scripture, the Word incarnate in Christ illumining darkened hearts and understanding. In clarifying the order of Scripture's use, Wesley demonstrates his insightfulness as a reader of

Scripture and spiritual director. While faith comes by hearing, it may also be confirmed by reading, meditating, and in conversation with others.

> With regard to the former, [their proper order] we may observe there is a kind of order wherein God himself is generally pleased to use these means in bringing a sinner to salvation. A stupid, senseless wretch is going on his way not having God in all his thoughts, when comes upon him unawares, perhaps by an awakening sermon or conversation, perhaps by some awful providence; or it may be an immediate stroke of his convicting Spirit, without any outward means at all. Having now a desire to flee from the wrath to come, he purposely goes to hear how it may be done. If he finds a preacher who speaks to his heart, he is amazed, and begins "searching the Scriptures," whether these things are so. The more he hears and reads, the more convinced he is; and the more he meditates thereon day and night. Perhaps he finds some other book that explains and enforces what he has heard and read in Scripture. And by all these means the arrows of conviction sink deeper into his soul.[51]

In addition to order there is also a manner that is appropriate for the use of Scripture and recommending its benefits. Wesley supposes that reading Scripture by a nonbeliever might also include listening and engaging in conversation with others. On the other hand, a believing person burdened by the weight of sin might be encouraged to mediate, read, and converse with others who share a similar spiritual condition.[52] Wesley emphasizes the importance of the work of divine providence and the Holy Spirit that go before and open the way within the life of humanity. In other words, there is a practical wisdom appropriate to the use of Scripture as a means of grace; a capacity for discerning connections between God's Word in Scripture and the work of God's Spirit in the diverse circumstances of ministry.

Cultivating this kind of practical wisdom requires humility, the sense that God as source and end is greater than any means and cannot be limited. For this reason, a right use of the means according to proper method is not an end in itself, but is a way to wait upon the Holy Spirit who works to renovate humanity through participation in the righteousness and holiness of Christ. As Wesley warns, "Beware you do not stick in the work itself; if you do, it is all lost labour. Nothing short of God can satisfy your soul. Therefore eye him in all, through all, and above all."[53]

Wesley's discussion of "searching the Scriptures" helps us to see that God matters in the use of the Bible to engender faith that turns the church toward God. When the use of Scripture, as a means of grace, is treated as the end itself, its true end—coming to know and love God—will be displaced by other ends to which God is subordinated as an instrumental means. Yet if the use of Scripture is reduced to a means of pursuing ends other than God, it will become a mere form of religion—while lacking its power. And if the use of Scripture becomes a means for producing results, it is no longer oriented by faith that waits for the work of divine grace. In other words, when faith that awaits the grace of God is displaced by a desire to pursue ends other than knowing and loving God, the use of Scripture is separated from its true scope and goal. Moreover, when God and the use of Scripture are divided, preaching is reduced to the expertise of technicians who work by means of privatized faith and productive technical reason. Thus, when God's Word and God's work have been separated—the disjunction of grace and nature—we have lost the sense of Scripture as a means through which the Spirit imparts the wisdom and power of Christ, which is our salvation.

Contrary to the standard account which views Wesley as either a pragmatic conservative or liberal revisionist, his view of the use of Scripture as a means of grace was shaped by orthodoxy and the teaching of the Church of England. Scripture functions "sacramentally," as a channel of truth and goodness that engenders praise for the gifts of creation and redemption; what Outler describes as "high church evangelicalism."[54] Wesley concludes with an exhortation to praise God:

> Lastly, after you have used any of these [means of grace], take care how you value yourself thereon; how you congratulate yourself as having done some great thng. This is turning all into poison. Think, "If God was not there, what does this avail? Have I not been adding sin to sin? How long, O Lord! Save, or I perish! O lay not this sin to my charge!" If God was not there, if his love flowed into your heart, you have forgot, as it were, the outward work. You see, you know, you feel, God is all in all. Be abased. Sink down before him. Give him all praise. Let God "in all things be glorified through Christ Jesus." Let "all your bones cry out," "My song shall be always of the lovingkindness of the Lord: With my mouth will I ever be telling of thy truth, from one generation to another."[55]

God matters in preaching. Wesley's turn "back to the future" encourages us to seek the knowledge of Scripture through which the living Word guides and nourishes the church on the "right and perfect way" toward holiness and happiness in God. The 1562 edition of the *Book of Homilies* exhorts its readers:

> There can be nothing either more necessary or profitable, than the knowledge of Holy Scripture; forasmuch as in it is contained God's true word, setting forth his glory, and also man's duty. And there is not truth nor doctrine, necessary for our justification and everlasting salvation, but that is, or may be, drawn out of that fountain or well of truth. . . . And as drink is pleasant to them that be dry, and meat to them that be hungry; so is the reading, hearing, searching, and studying of Holy Scripture, to them that be desirous to know God, or themselves, and to do his will. . . . These books therefore, ought to be much in our hands, in our eyes, in our mouths, but most of all in our hearts. For the Scripture of God is the heavenly meat of our souls; the hearing and keeping of it maketh us blessed, sanctifieth us, and maketh us holy; it turneth our souls; it is a light and lantern to our feet; it is a sure, steadfast, and everlasting intstrument of salvation. . . . The words of Holy Scripture be called words of everlasting life; for they be God's instrument, ordained for the same purpose. They have power to turn, through God's promise; and to be effectual through God's assitance; and being received in a faithful heart, they have an heavenly spiritual working in them.[56]

CHAPTER 4

SPEAKING THE TRUTH IN LOVE

Writing in the preface to the 1746 edition of *Sermons on Several Occasions*, John Wesley states that, given the nature of his training, background, and interests, the sermons may not meet the expectations of readers whose curiosity would lead them to look for other things.

> Nothing here appears in an elaborate, elegant, or oratorical dress. If it had been my desire or design to write this, my leisure would not permit. But in truth I, at present designed nothing less, for I now write (as I generally speak) and populum—to the bulk of mankind—to those who neither relish nor understand the art of speaking, but how notwithstanding are competent judges of those truths which are necessary to present and future happiness.[1]

Wesley then identifies his purpose: "I design plain truth for plain people." In practice, this means an avoidance of philosophical niceties and speculation, intricate reasoning, and ostensive displays of learning. The only learning Wesley desires to demonstrate is a knowledge of Scripture. Speaking by means of the patterns and sounds of common speech, he pledges to refrain from the use of technical terms familiar to those educated in theological things in order to interest and engage those who are not. Wesley claims that he aims to "forget" what he has learned about theology in order to communicate what lies at the heart of theology—the knowledge and love of God—without entangling himself or his listeners in the presuppositions and prejudices of others. In other words, a kind of "learned ignorance." And this is for the sake of discovering and speaking the "naked truths" of the gospel. Albert Outler writes of Wesley's claims:

> Wesley's stake in this sort of learning and his "concealment" of it came from his passion for a message that would gather into itself the riches of both Christian and classical traditions and that still could be shared with his "plain people."

This is what lies behind and beneath the surface rhetoric of the sermons including his claim to be *homo unius libri*. It is this veiled background which, nevertheless, gives the sermons themselves an extra dimension of depth and originality rarely found in typical popularizers.[2]

Outler explains that his reference to "typical popularizers" means preachers who accommodate themselves to the limitations of culture and tend to work with less care for the Christian tradition as a whole. The strength of their preaching is characterized by a kind of fluency with biblical language and mixed with a self-confidence that tends to rely on personal experience and charisma. In what may seem to some as a surprising judgment, Outler distances Wesley from such popularizers, emphasizing the consistency of his theological convictions by comparing him with exemplars such as Luther, Chrysostom, and Augustine, theologically oriented preachers who spoke out of an overflow of Christian knowledge and wisdom derived from extensive engagement with Scripture. The message of preaching *is* the medium, just as preaching's message and medium are shaped by the language and truth of the Bible.

My interest in this chapter is to situate Wesley with the Anglican preaching tradition as an evangelical and catholic voice in a time when more and more theologians were thinking out their theology—the knowledge of God and things of God—in sermons, or "homiletic theology." Wesley was neither a rationalist (reason without revelation) nor enthusiast (revelation above reason); rather, his preaching unites the intellect and will, knowledge with love, in faithful response to the truth and goodness of God revealed in Jesus Christ; a form of theologically oriented, "popular" preaching that reached thousands of people over the course of more than six decades.[3] Wesley's preaching was the fruit of prayerful study and diligent interpretation of the truths of Scripture that were communicated in a plain style characterized by clarity of thought and simplicity of devotion. At the same time, this elevation of the Word was accompanied by a great hunger for the church's sacramental life and rehabilitation of doctrine for renewing Christian existence in the knowledge and love of God.[4]

I suspect that one of the most challenging obstacles to appreciating Wesley's "popular" sermons as theological discourse may be the North American tradition of populism, which has its roots in nineteenth-century revivalism. For example, Brooks Holifield writes of American Methodists who

> largely ignored Wesley's Anglican admiration for patristic sources, his sacramentalism, and his liturgical piety; they appropriated his anti-Calvinism, his revivalism, and his perfectionism, and they reshaped even that by filtering it through the lens of Scottish philosophy, mental science, and the free-wheeling denominational polemics of American popular Christianity.[5]

Mark Noll has argued that the frontier revivals of the 1770s and 1780s marked the emergence of a voluntarist, individualist, and sectarian kind of Protestantism now associated by many with evangelicalism. Newly established American Christians identified themselves with essential qualities of America's founding, as Noll observes, "the democratic, republican, commonsensical, liberal, and providential conceptions by which the founders had identified America." Thus for most of the nineteenth century, American Protestantism continued to be aligned with the American political project and its new market economy, which provided a welcoming environment for the moralistic zeal of revivalism that served to legitimate the individuated market and the myth of rational individualism and individual choice.[6]

This "democratization" of Christianity imbibed deeply of the revolutionary spirit, with the ministry of Charles Finney in the 1830s being the climax of a process that had begun a half century earlier. Finney inspired a "Copernican revolution," which made religion exciting and "audience centered," scorning traditional religion for producing dull and ineffective communication, borrowing instead from the rhetorical techniques of populist politicians, and significantly, shifting the emphasis from the truth to be communicated to the effective communication of that truth, thereby changing the subject of preaching from message to method.[7] Finney's popular methods were not primarily informed by the church's trinitarian doctrine and way of life as adhered to by a Jonathan Edwards or John Wesley, but rather by a "commonsense theism" with its vigorous empiricism that privileged the facts of the Bible and the facts of individual consciousness by which he presumed to judge Christian tradition and history for their contemporary usefulness.[8]

This commonsense rationality was drawn toward scientific predictability that is reflected in Finney's *Lectures on Revivals of Religion* (1835) that set forth reliable laws that could be activated by reason as *techne* within a cause and effect religious world, analogous to, but abstracted from the natural, sensuous world: "The connection between the right use of means for a revival of and a revival is as philosophically [i.e., scientifically] sure as between right use of means to raise grain and a crop of wheat. I believe in fact it is more certain, and there are few instances of failure."[9] In other words, it was possible to "effect" successful revival while remaining indifferent toward or departing from the doctrinal and liturgical tradition.

The distinctively American character of Finney's pragmatic populism is evinced by his insistence that whatever cannot be made immediately useful is not preaching the gospel. In his zeal to reach lost souls, moreover, Finney's definition of what constitutes "useful" and "practical" was increasingly shaped by a form of biblicism grounded in private judgment and personal experience, a Christian antitraditionalism which, while representing liberation from the Christian past to pursue the "new" and "improved," also tended toward a form of "Christianity without Christ."[10] Hughes Old has named this type of preaching "the Great American School," describing it as encouraging an optimistic, progressive habit of mind that assumed that simple solutions could be found for complex problems, fusing freedom of conscience with simple truths from the Bible by use of commonsense and enlightened reason. "One admits the Great American School had a rather weak understanding of Scripture. . . . The school was so completely absorbed in revival and reform that Scripture was of interest only insofar as it could point the way to these goals."[11] In other words, means and ends were divided and confused.

Finney's pragmatism shifted the center of Christian virtue as it was understood by preachers such as Wesley or Edwards from the knowledge and love of God through divine grace and the gift of faith, to an emphasis on obedience to God's law, moral self-governance, the freedom of the will, and a natural capacity for exercising moral choice to obey God. According to Timothy Weber, Finney's idiosyncratic "Arminianized/Calvinism" taught that anyone who wanted to could be saved, an individual decision that could be "worked up as well as prayed down" by use of empirically derived methods and measures: aggressive advertising, gospel music that heightened emotions, and sophisticated organization and planning.[12]

By placing primary emphasis on human agency, voluntarism, and the will in making a decision for Christ, revivalists such as Finney helped along the "sanctification" of choice, thereby preparing the way for the pleasures of modern consumerism that helped to redefine Christianity in terms of the marketplace of felt needs and desires. As effecting revival became an end in itself, larger matters of reform and the renovation of life were increasingly neglected. The emphasis on the right choice of means and their effective use to achieve immediate results contributed to a theology and ethic of consumption, production, and economic efficiency, replacing the providential activity of God that is discerned within a common life constituted by a tradition of doctrine, devotion, and discipline.[13]

Thus in its neglect of truth and theological wisdom due to preoccupations with the effectiveness of human communicators rather than the efficacy of God speaking, such preaching arguably conveys a sense of God's absence by its content, form, and style. Interestingly, during the past generation such forms of "effective" communication have been increasingly promoted as "cutting-edge," "state of the art," and admired for their novelty and innovation. However, as William Willimon observes, the prevailing tendency to divide the message and method of preaching; a preoccupation with "how to" communicate effectively—but without sufficient attention to the theological convictions that constitute preaching as a Christian practice—is a contemporary manifestation of the nineteenth-century shift in the focus of sermons from the pulpit to the people; from the theological convictions of the church to the immediate, personal concerns of the congregation and its relevance to culture, the economy, and the nation. Lacking the particular theological substance and scope of Christian convictions, preachers will continue to be tempted to use forms of speech that render God without a people and a people without God.[14] In other words, without God the sermon is easily reduced to a moralistic or motivational talk delivered to an audience of listeners, rather than an assembly called by the Spirit to worship the Triune God in communion with the whole body of Christ.

Nor is it a coincidence that during the nineteenth century rhetorical form and style played a more prominent role in preaching than did theology; a homiletic characteristic that remains popular among both mainline and evangelical churches. James Kay provides an insightful overview of changes that occurred in preaching during this time. Arguably, the most significant was the separation of preaching from doctrine and its regrounding in the framework of rhetoric. Kay argues that the rise of "pulpit eloquence" was due to the influence of George Campbell, Hugh Blair, and John Witherspoon, scholars who claimed that homiletics was most naturally understood as a branch of rhetoric. What this meant for preaching, however, was that rhetoric was regarded as the constant and theology the variable. "Indeed, beginning with Witherspoon, homiletics in America, has generally operated within a primarily, rhetorical frame of reference. . . . Pulpit eloquence, mindful of its audience, packages and delivers Christian doctrine."[15]

This predominately rhetorical approach remained popular in North America until it began to wane during latter decades of the twentieth century when it was "revived" by populist "mega" churches that measure homiletic effectiveness in terms of quantifiable results and the satisfaction of listener demand through exciting, entertaining, and "practically relevant" communication. At the same time, the contemporary revival of "Finneyism" has also manifested many of the temptations associated with its methods; the fostering of self-centered, egotistic, and narcissistic spiritualities that trivialize the gospel by marketing it to consumers. If preaching is not adjusted to listeners' "deeply felt needs," a preacher risks the dissatisfaction of hearers who, in the contemporary marketplace of religious desire, are free to shop for a more personally accommodating speaker and personally relevant message.[16]

When homiletic and evangelization strategies are determined by the turn to the listener, rather than the theological content and purpose of Scripture— God's truth and goodness—the rhetoric of preaching is made extrinsic to the subject matter of preaching—God incarnate. In other words, without the practical wisdom of doctrine as its guide, or rule, preaching can be used as a "technological device" for producing predetermined results—rather than an embodied witness to the truth of the gospel by which the Spirit orients the church to hear and be formed by the Word, or God speaking.[17]

Popular Preaching in England

In committing himself to preach *ad populum*, Wesley resisted accommodating his preaching to a rhetorical frame of reference. As he writes in the preface to the 1788 edition of sermons, "I could even now write floridly . . . as even the admired Dr. [Hugh] Blair. But I dare not. . . . I dare no more write in a 'fine style' than wear a fine coat. . . . I cannot relish French oratory—I despise it from my heart. . . . I am still for plain, sound English."[18] On the other hand, Wesley's desire to speak in plain English should not be taken as representing a turn toward preaching that is either anti-intellectual or nontheological in its content or purpose. In other words, Wesley's sermons were not pragmatic examples of doing "what works" for maximizing results, since he describes the nature of the sermons in theological terms, "Every serious man who peruses these will therefore see in the clearest manner what those doctrines are which I embrace and teach as the essentials of true religion."[19] For Wesley, the "essentials of true religion" unite knowledge and love, healing the separation of intellect and will by the gift of divine grace. For this reason, knowing and loving the truth of God matters in preaching, since we cannot love what we do not know, and we are only happy when we love what we know. As Wesley writes in his sermon "The Unity of the Divine Being":

> It is in consequence of our knowing God loves us that we love him, and love our neighbor as ourselves. . . . The love of Christ constrains us, not only to be harmless, to do no ill to our neighbor, but be useful, to be "zealous unto good works" as we have time to do good unto all men and be patterns to all of true genuine morality, of justice, mercy, and truth. This is religion, and this is happiness, the happiness for which we were made. This begins when we begin to know God, by the teaching of his Spirit. As soon as the Father reveals his Son in our hearts, and the Son reveals the Father, the love of God is shed abroad in our hearts; then, and not till then, we are happy. We are first happy in the consciousness of his favor, which indeed is better than the life itself; next in the constant communion with the Father, and with his Son, Jesus Christ; then in all the heavenly tempers which he hath wrought in us by his Spirit.[20]

Stephen Long's discussion of Wesley's moral theology, the unity of doctrine and life, shows the limitations of modernity's reliance upon technical method and thinking, which, when aligned with will-to-power, loses the richness of language and truth as disclosed in the narrative context and practices that orient the church to God: "The more Christianity seeks relevance to the technical rationality in which modern Western culture ends, the more it forsakes any orienting power in the world." He continues:

> The modern era ends with the dominance of technology which is characterized by the repetition of the obsolete and the emergence of the "new and improved." These notions have allowed technology to shape being, yet the recurring cycle of obsolescence/new creation is itself part of a historical tradition . . . technology is the completion of the Western metaphysical tradition, a tradition that ends in nihilism. . . . Nihilism's death of god puts theology out of work [which] is to deny theology any shaping force in history. . . . Like a virus that works on one's operating system, mimicking its functions, nihilism and its technological fascination overtakes Christianity, rendering it inoperative.[21]

A major symptom of this virus is evinced by contemporary forms of popular evangelistic preaching that tend toward moralistic, therapeutic deism that "works" through the application of pragmatic principles derived from reason and experience—but with neither the understanding nor desire intrinsic to knowing and loving God through the illuminating work of the Spirit. In other words, the "effective" preacher has become an agent of instrumental reason who speaks in the place of God by means of technological mastery and skill.[22]

For Wesley, however, evangelization that is not oriented toward transformation of the whole person in love with God and others through participation in the human righteousness of Christ would not be seen as fully Christian. Left behind are the virtues and habits of "true religion" that are received through the public reading and hearing of Scripture, confessing the truth of the creeds, participating in the liturgy and Eucharist, adhering to the doctrine and discipline of the Anglican Church, and following the General Rules of Methodist Societies.[23]

The move to reenvision preaching within a rhetorical frame of reference was part of a larger shift that led to forms of thought that centered on the arbitrary power of the will and personal preferences, rather than a desire for truth and goodness. Wesley did not view the will as an arbitrary freedom to choose, but rather understood it as reasonable desire that is ordered to the true and moved by the good. Rather than mere power or ability to choose without the truth of a specific object, the will is moved by the intellect toward what it knows, which in the case of the subject matter of living faith—the Triune God—is mediated by Word, sacrament, and the means of grace. For this reason, the will discovers and pursues the good only as the understanding discovers, or is discovered by, the truth. Preached truth promotes true religion; the knowledge and love of God.[24]

Knowledge of God and knowledge of the self are inseparable, as are love of God and neighbor. Wesley interpreted the eternal law as "right reason" in light of the glory revealed by the Incarnation; by the mind of Christ we are transformed and in which we participate by faith and the disposition of love to know God and see reality.

> Now this law is an incorruptible picture of the high and holy One that inhabiteth eternity. It is he whom in his essence no man hath seen or can see, made visible to men and angels. It is the face of God unveiled; God manifested to his creatures as they are able to bear it; manifested to give and not to destroy life; that they may see God and live. . . . Yea, in some sense we may apply to this law what the Apostle says of his Son—it is "the streaming forth" or outbeaming "of his glory, the express image of his person." . . . The law of God is all virtues in one, in such a shape to be beheld with open face by all those whose eyes God hath enlightened. What is the law but divine virtue and wisdom assuming a visible form? What is it but the original ideas of truth and good, which were lodged in the uncreated mind from eternity, now drawn forth and clothed with such a vehicle as to appear even in human understanding?[25]

The Christian life for Wesley is primarily a function of knowledge rather than will. Rather than an instrument of choice, he saw the will as the internal and external movement of rational desire, a unity of understanding and affection ordered to the truth and goodness desired by human creatures and revealed by Christ. Long's discussion of Wesley's moral theology helps us to see that if God matters in preaching, understanding the will as a free power to choose cannot provide a sufficient theological basis for proclaiming the Word of God. The will is moved by the truth that the intellect sees, just as the intellect is moved by the good desired by the will. If doctrine and life are divided, a preacher may be ignorant but can still be good. However, the measure of this goodness will be sincerity and authenticity—rather than the knowledge of faith illumined by God's self-revelation in Christ that helps faith to understand what it believes.[26]

Wesley's emphasis on doctrine and truth did not fit well within the framework of American revivalism with its turn to the listener and emphasis on sin, choice, and exercise of the will and sentiment, since he understood reason as the source of knowledge rather than experience or scientific predictability. Because the mind participates in the mind of God through the illumination of the Second Person of the Trinity—the vision of Christ—the renewal of humanity in the divine image presupposes the doctrinal context of Trinity and Incarnation. Wesley writes:

> How little is understood in the Christian world! Yea, or this enlightened age, wherein it is taken for granted, the world is wiser than ever it was from the beginning of the world. Among all our discoverers, who has discovered this? How few either among the learned or the unlearned? . . . Beware of taking anything else, or anything else less than this for religion. Not anything else; do not imagine an outward form, a round of duties, both in public and private, is religion. Do not suppose that honesty, justice, and whatever is called morality (though excellent in its place) is religion.[27]

Rather than interpreting Wesley in light of the American revivalist tradition, it will be more appropriate to place him within a tradition of popular preaching reaching back to the late medieval church, which was renewed within the practical context of the Church of England as constituted by the *Book of Homilies, Book of Common Prayer,* and *Articles of Religion.* For example, from the late 1540s until the death of Edward VI in 1553—the origins of the Protestant Church of England—a committed company of preachers traveled the countryside of England, proclaiming the Word to evangelize and edify popular audiences. Christopher Haigh has described these preachers "as remarkable a group of evangelists as can ever be seen."[28] While preaching at Grimsthorpe in Lincolnshire, Hugh Latimer, arguably the most influential among the first generation of Anglican popular preachers, confirmed his personal inclination for this task.

I have a manner of teaching which is very tedious to them that be learned. I am wont ever to repeat those things which I have said before, which are nothing pleasant to the learned; but it is no matter, I care not for them; I seek more the profit of these who be ignorant, than to please learned men. (*Works*, 1:341)

Popular preaching in sixteenth-century England wove together elements and emphases of both the old and the new, the known and the unknown in religion, devotion, and life to create common ground for the gospel, a middle way between the extreme positions held by traditionalists and radicals. This strategy enabled homiletic discourse to engage or overlap with much that was familiar to audiences, thus softening the impact of religious change. Although their aim was to reach a wide audience, sermons called for commitment deeper than mere outward conformity, selectively employing biblical language to remove obstacles that could prevent listeners from receiving their consensus-forming message of living faith and love.

David Steinmetz has written of the reforming perspective of the first generation among sixteenth-century Protestants, a vision of "traditioned change."

What set the Protestant message off from the medieval tradition was not the uniqueness of its questions or the newness of its sources. What set it off was the angle of vision from which these traditional sources were read and evaluated. The Christian past was not so much rejected by the Protestant reformers as refashioned in the light of a different and competing vision of its development and continuing significance.[29]

The fashioning of a renewed church in Edwardian England was shaped by the implementation of Thomas Cranmer's liturgical reforms.[30] The work of John Wall clarifies the role of common worship for the Edwardian commonwealth and helps to situate popular preaching against the background of Archbishop Cranmer's larger program. Wall persuasively argues that the distinctive marks of the Edwardian church, the *Ecclesia Anglicana*, included its recovery of the Bible in the vernacular as a living text addressed to English folk; its creation of a vernacular discipline of common prayer as the appropriate context for reading and preaching Scripture. By placing the prayer book, basic Christian texts, and liturgical events at the center of religious discourse,

Cranmer sought the transformation of England into a Christian common-wealth through participation in Christ through living faith and the active love of neighbor as the way of citizenship into God's kingdom.[31] The theological significance of liturgical reform was affirmed in the preface to the 1549 *Book of Common Prayer*.

> There was never anything by the wit of man so well devised or so sure estab-lished, which in continuance of time hath not been corrupted, as among other things, it may plainly appear by the common prayers in the Church, commonly called Divine Service. The first and original ground whereof if a man would search out by the ancient Fathers, he shall find that the same was not ordained but of a good purpose and for a great advancement of godliness. For they so ordered the matter that the whole Bible (or the greatest part thereof) should be read over once every year; intending thereby that the clergy, and especially such as were ministers in the congregation, should be stirred up to godliness them-selves, and be more able to exhort others by wholesome doctrine, and to confute them that were adversaries to the truth; and further that the people (by daily reading of Holy Scripture in the Church) might continually profit more and more in the knowledge of God and be more inflamed with the love of his true religion.[32]

The practical wisdom of Cranmer's program is confirmed by the work of Christopher Marsh who challenges the emphasis placed by revisionist scholars on the inescapable hold of late medieval Christianity over the English church and its assertion that Protestantism held little appeal for ordinary people.[33] Marsh argues that the radical distinction between the old and the new did not predominate in the way that revisionists tend to portray in their assertions that key Protestant doctrines were too demanding and dangerously divisive; that an emphasis on the printed vernacular Bible was misplaced in a largely illiterate society; that godly attempts to reform popular practices inspired contempt. Marsh perceptively notes that not all English Reformers were cast in the mold of a John Hooper who adopted radical, uncompromising strategies.[34] For example, in composing the *Book of Common Prayer*, Cranmer retained certain ceremonies and traditions (including vestments) insisting, "Lest the people not having yet learned Christ, should be deterred by too extensive innovation from embracing his religion." He therefore designed the practices of the prayer book to be a middle path between "those addicted to the old customs and those so new-fangled that they would innovate all things."[35]

Popular Anglican preaching is best understood against the background of Cranmer's more gradualist and moderate liturgical and pastoral strategies that aimed to convert the nation to evangelical faith and a life of love for God and neighbor. An additionally significant element of the Edwardian church was the use of English as the medium for its liturgical life. As Wall concludes, "Thus the translation of the Bible into English and the transformation of diverse Latin rites into a life of common prayer in the vernacular through a single use for all English folk became vehicles for realizing that new sense of God's actions in the present life of the nation."[36] In 1549 Cranmer declared this theological purpose for a new book of common prayers.

> And moreover, whereas St. Paul would have such language spoken to the people in the Church as they might understand and have profit by hearing the same, the service in this Church of England these many years hath been read in Latin to the people, which they understand not, so that they have heard with their ears only and their heart, spirit and mind have not been edified thereby.[37]

King remarks, "Gone forever was the supremacy of the medieval mass, which had been celebrated out of the sight of the people in a language they could not understand." This union of common prayer through common language promoted a communal dialogue between a speaking, summoning God and a listening, responding people; biblically mediated godly conversation replaced the medieval distinction between priest and people.[38] The 1552 Act of Uniformity, announcing the implementation of a revised *Book of Common Prayer*, refers to its "very godly order . . . to be used in the mother tongue within the Church of England . . . very comfortable to all good people desiring to live in Christian conversation . . . by common prayers, due using of the sacraments and frequent preaching of the Word of God with the devotion of its hearers."[39]

Latimer is arguably the outstanding exemplar of the colloquial style among Edwardian preachers.[40] His plain style of preaching, in imitation of plain Bible English, is accommodated to facilitate conversation with and conversion of the broadest possible audience—universal and catholic—granting his sermons a flavor prompting historians to categorize him as a "typically medieval preacher."[41] Indeed, Latimer's popularizing style, marked by its picturesque imagery, earthy diction, and figures of speech, enabled him to communicate through direct, concrete, unadorned, passionate language that displayed obvious continuities with the best of patristic and medieval preaching *ad populum*.[42] H. O. Taylor describes Latimer's use of language.

> He drew his convictions from the Scriptures as spontaneously as he drew the illustrations of them from the world around him. His sermons reflected and absorbed the habits, the demands, the hardships, the very implements and incidents of English life, all straight from the preacher to his audience. Here indeed was an English Gospeller whose thoughts and phrases seemed to echo Wyclif: "right prelating is busy labouring, and not lording" might have been Wyclif's or Latimer's.[43]

The issue of language and style in popular preaching was not merely a social concern but reflected doctrinal and moral commitments bound up with the reform of church and society in England. A challenge faced by the Edwardian preachers was being able to bridge the gap between "high and low," the capacity for opening new lines of communication that would reconcile learned piety with lay devotion. This required a discovery of plain, fitting speech that held to Scripture's message for the enactment of lively faith, a form of sacred rhetoric that would engage diverse audiences with language sufficiently persuasive to overcome habits of passivity or resistance to reform. As Cranmer wrote in the preface to the *Great Bible*,

> Here may all manner of persons, men, women, young, old, learned, unlearned, rich, poor, priests, laymen, lords, ladies, officers, tenants, and mean men, virgins, wives, widows, lawyers, merchants, artificers, husbandmen, and all manner of persons, of what estate or condition soever they be, may in THIS BOOK learn all things, that they ought to believe, what they ought to do, and what they should not do, as well concerning Almighty God, as also concerning themselves, and all others.[44]

Popular preachers such as Latimer were exceptionally qualified to address the challenge of spreading reform on the ground level in England. Their potential effectiveness with common folk was enhanced by a plain manner of speaking that deprofessionalized and popularized the basic teaching of a renewed church that enabled them to engage listeners in a way uncommon for bishops and high-ranking ecclesiastical or university officials. Such vernacular preaching by a learned preacher was potentially subversive, since its wide appeal presented an alternative to what was typically expected within the late medieval church, an expectation caricatured by Erasmus in *The Praise of Folly*.[45]

> Tell me now, is there any comedian or pitchman you would rather see than these men when they orate in these sermons, imitating quite absurdedly but still very amusingly what the rhetoricians have handed down about the way to make a speech? Good lord! How they gesticulate, how fittingly they vary the tone of their voice, how they croon, how they strut, continually changing their facial expressions, drowning out everything with their shouts! And the mysterious secret of this oratorical artistry is passed down personally from one friar to another.

Humble Speech

Here it will be helpful to consider briefly the Augustinian renaissance in sixteenth- and seventeenth-century England that was promoted by Christian humanists, especially Erasmus, and embraced by both Catholic and Protestant reformers: a renewal marked by a return to a form of sacred rhetoric modeled on the plain style of Scripture while still remaining appropriate to its sacred subject.[46] The text that was most influential during this time was Augustine's *De Doctrina Christiana*, or "Christian Teaching."

Augustine concludes the church's first handbook of pastoral theology in the following manner: "I, for my part, give thanks to our God that in these four books I have set out to the best of my poor ability, not what sort of pastor I am myself, lacking many of the necessary qualities as I do, but what sort of pastor should be who is eager to toil away, not only for his own sake but for others, in the teaching of sound Christian doctrine."[47] For Augustine, preaching is not simply a call to believe something, to learn something, or to do something; it is to be made a truthful witness to Christ through knowing and loving the incarnate Word who shapes our lives and gives shape to all the words we speak. In Augustine's words, the pastor is to be transformed into an "eloquent sermon," a performative way of reading, speaking and living that invites others to loving conversation with the Father, Son and Holy Spirit (DDC, IV.27.59). The paradox of preaching as a pastoral practice is that in listening to and learning from God more than people, pastors are better equipped to speak in a manner that assists others to hear the voice of God who speaks to call, form, and guide a pilgrim church through time.

The whole of *De doctrina christiana* can be read as an extended performance of Christian speech, since Augustine's aim was the conversion of his readers and the cultivation of the necessary wisdom, dispositions, and affections for hearing and speaking the truth of God's Word. The robust theology of providence and divine grace that underlies books I–III informs Augustine's description of Christian preaching as the effect of the Word and Spirit, a capacity for speaking and hearing is produced by neither ingenuity nor skill, but rather is received and returned through the church's self-offering of praise and thanksgiving to the Triune God.[48]

Book IV is the goal or end to which the whole of *De doctrina christiana* moves: the proclamation of the truth of God whose knowledge and love re-forms the church into the likeness of Christ through practices of doxology, discipleship, and devotion. Because God is the Divine Orator, the plain style of Scripture mediates the rhetoric of God; while at the same time God's rhetorical aim is the saving intention of Scripture; the truth and goodness revealed in Christ and made effectual through the Spirit.[49] God teaching through Scripture—knowledge inspired by love—shapes preaching's content, form, and style.

Augustine's pastoral teaching orients us to the truth and excellence of God's saving wisdom that is eloquently communicated in Christ and in the Spirit for reordering human understanding and desire to creation's final end. Acknowledging that rhetoric plays a limited but appropriate role in serving the truth, Augustine emphasizes the gift of God's rhetoric, the wisdom of Love incarnate, who with compassion humbled himself to become our neighbor, and whose loving obedience to the Father overcame our desire to control others through the power of words. "It is our love of God which is a reflection of God's love for us and is a transforming power which makes us conform to the beauty of the divine nature."[50]

The divine teaching inscribed in the scriptural narrative has the character of wisdom and eloquence which, rather then teaching things—since knowledge puffs up—transforms by the light of Christ's wisdom and the power of his goodness. Scripture's content and form are thus one in communicating God's truth through the love that creates and redeems all things.[51] Moreover, the truth and goodness revealed by Christ's lowliness is the focus of the church's contemplation and imitation.[52] In an analogous manner, the living Word condescends through the mediation of Scripture to become incarnate in preachers whose being, life, and speech bear witness to God's humble speech, or *Sermo Humilis*.

Erich Auerbach has traced the roots of the humble word or *Sermo Humilis* to the Church Fathers, with Augustine being its most outstanding proponent in his defense and practice of the biblical writers' plain, humble style.[53] Ironically, *Humilis* is related to humus, the soil, and literally means low lying, of small stature, an allusion to the plowman-preacher who embodies the humility of the incarnation in speech and life, a voluntary humiliation illustrated by a life on earth among the lowest social classes, among the materially and spiritually poor, thus reflecting the whole character of Christ's acts and teachings.[54] Not simply a form of "packaging," the plain style is an expression of a mind illumined by God's wisdom incarnate in Christ.

The purpose of such humility is to make the message of the Word, especially its spiritual truth, clear and available to all without intimidating or repelling the unlearned. In such popular preaching the lowly, earthy style that was made flesh in Christ and inscribed in Scripture is able to overcome barriers to evoke a world of divine glory accommodating itself to the ordinary through incarnate wisdom and love.[55]

Peter Brown has written of the manner in which bishops like Augustine presented Christianity to the ancient world, offering a universal way of salvation that was gathering all nations and classes into its bosom, *populari sinu*. The Bible itself, with its layers of meaning and sense, was a microcosm, a textual world of the social and intellectual diversity to be found in Christian churches. Augustine exclaimed, "Its plain language and simple style make it accessible to all . . . this book stands out alone on so high a peak of authority and yet can draw the crowds to the embrace of its inspired simplicity." Augustine bore witness to the incarnate Christ who indwells Scripture and the church to create a Christian populism, simple words endowed with divine authority for large, unlearned segments of the empire.[56] Augustine therefore embodied a form of practical wisdom that communicated the bending, reaching, and embracing Word he proclaimed: the *Sermo Humilis*, or humble way of love that he had come to "see" in Christ with the eyes of his heart cleansed by the Word. *Sermo Humilis*, then, is a fitting expression for both the way and goal of this transformation.

This "catholic" use of Scripture in England sought to make the word of God accessible to the body of Christians as a whole—especially plain, common folk. A humble spirit and attentiveness to God were necessary for producing competent hearers, speakers, and doers of the Word—personal knowledge of the truth—as encouraged by the Edwardian *Homilies*.

> Read it [Holy Scripture] humbly, with a meke and a lowly harte, to thinet you maie glorifie God, and not your self, with the knowledge of it; and reade it not without daily praiying to God that he would directe your readying to good effecte; and take upon you to expounde it no further than you can plainly understande it. For, as St. Augustine saieth, the knowledge of Holy Scripture is a great, large, and high palace, but the door is verie lowe so the high and arrogant man cannot runne in, but he must stoupe lowe and humble hym self that shall entre into it ("Readying of Holy Scripture," 65).

The practical wisdom of Anglican popular preaching sheds light on Wesley's commitment to "plain truth for plain folk." Love does not forbid but rather requires plain speech, since the primary consideration is not who it is that speaks but the truth that is spoken. This commitment is set down in the minutes of the 1746 Methodist Conference, where a series of questions are devoted to the examination or "trying" of those who believed they were moved by the Spirit and called to preach. Interestingly, rather than focusing on pragmatic matters of skill, style, and method, the questions are concerned with a preacher's faith, love, and devotion, as well as the quality of one's knowledge, understanding, desire, judgment and discernment appropriate to God, the message of preaching, and the condition and circumstances of listeners. Required is the cultivation of virtue and practical wisdom that enables a preacher to "see" the world in light of God's work in Christ. This is why the truth of God matters in preaching.

> Do they know in whom they have believed?; Have they the love of God in their hearts?; Do they desire and seek nothing but God?; And are they holy in all manner of conversation?; Have they a clear understanding?; Have they a right judgment in the things of God?; Have they a just conception of the salvation by faith?; And has God given them any degree of utterance. Do they speak justly, readily, clearly? . . . Do they not only speak as generally either to convince or affect the hearts—but have any received remission of sins by their preaching— a clear and lasting sense of the love of God?; As long as these . . . marks unde- niably concur in any, we allow him to be called of God to preach. These we receive as sufficient evidence that he is moved thereto by the Holy Ghost.[57]

CHAPTER 5

THE WAY TO GOD

My aim to this point has been to show that John Wesley's robust, theologically oriented homiletic wisdom makes him well-suited for addressing the need to liberate preaching *and* preachers—"the preaching life"—from captivity to the "tyranny of the practical," which relegates theology and preaching to separate compartments of privatized faith and productive, technical reason.[1] Although this theory-practice split is valued by some for its instrumental "effectiveness," it effectively conveys a vision of reality that divides God and humanity, grace and nature, faith and reason, Scripture and life, the Word and human words. As a result, preaching is imprisoned within an autonomous, a-theological realm of human communication deeply inhospitable to the Spirit's gifts of faith, hope, and love that make us participants in God's good work.[2] In other words, God no longer matters in preaching.

Such forms of dualism betray in practice what Wesley described as a kind of "practical atheism," which values Christianity for its translatability into arrangements that depict God in utilitarian rather than doctrinal terms.[3] However, if the heart, mind, soul, and body are not oriented by the Spirit to the truth and goodness of Christ, our use of words, including the words of preaching, will easily become forms of self-assertion, expressions of "pseudo-reality" that subordinate truth to power.[4]

Following the wisdom of the Christian tradition, Wesley believed the completion of our human capacities requires the work of divine grace through the activity of Christ and the Holy Spirit within the worshiping life of the church. For theological reasons, then, "effective" communication is an insufficient goal for preaching, since "good" preaching is internally related and oriented to the end of knowing and loving the God of Jesus Christ. This matter of intention was significant for Wesley, since he understood pastoral ministry as serving ends essential for the life of the church: "glorifying God and saving souls

79

from death," to which he adds, "This is absolutely and indispensably necessary, before and above all things."[5] In other words, preaching is not an activity done for some other purpose not already intrinsic to itself as a practice by which the Spirit orients the church to hear and receive the Word in Scripture and to be formed in the mind of Christ. The Elizabethan *Book of Homilies* states that the reading of Scripture bears fruit when we become what we read:

> And, to be short, there is noting that more maintaineth godliness of the mind, and driveth away ungodliness, than doth the continual reading or hearing of God's word, if it be joined with a godly mind, and a good affection to know and follow God's will. For withough a single eye, pure intent, and good mind, nothing is allowed for good before God.[6]

In addition to intention—the devotion of all we are and do to God— Wesley believed pastoral ministry requires a singular attention to God: "If his eye be single, his whole body, if his whole soul, his whole work will be full of light which the illumination of divine revelation, the 'God who commanded light to shine out of darkness' will shine in his heart; will direct him in all his ways, will give him to see the travail of his soul, and be satisfied." On the other hand, separating the means of ministry from God blurs the Creator-creature distinction, a condition in which "his whole body, his whole soul, will be full of darkness, even such as issues from the bottomless pit . . . neither can he hope will there be any fruit of his labours."[7]

In addressing the matter of affection and desire, Wesley notes that the work of the Holy Spirit will dispose a minister to delight in "be[ing] a steward of the mysteries of God, and shepherd of the souls for whom Christ died," and "to be endued with an eminent measure of love to God, and love to all his brethren; a love of the same kind, but in degree far beyond that of ordinary Christians."[8] Just as the presence and work of the Holy Spirit orders human intentions and affections to God, so does the Spirit illumine the intellect and move the will toward the truth and goodness of Christ through prayerful attentiveness to Scripture. Again, as the homilies exhort readers:

> Let us hear, read, and know thes holy rules, injunctions, and statutes of our Christian religion, and upon that we have made profession to God at our

baptism. Let us with fear and reverence lay up, in the chest of our hearts, these necessary and fruitful lessons; let us night and day muse, and have mediation and contemplation in them; let us ruminate, and as it were, chew the cud, that we may have the sweet juice, spiritual effect, marrow, kernel, taste, comfort, and consolation of them. . . . Let us pray to God, the only Author of these heavenly studies, that we may speak, think, believe, live, and depart hence, according to the wholesome doctrine and verities of them.[9]

Wesley's sermons express a scripturally informed way of thinking and speaking that springs from faith and works through love to participate in God's goodness and happiness: "As faith is in order to love, so love is in order to goodness—and so also goodness is in order to blessedness."[10] Moreover, the faithful proclamation of God's promises—communicated in the God's Word to Israel and fulfilled in God's Word incarnate—springs from the church's first-order liturgical enactment of the Word mediated by Scripture.[11] The language of preaching—speaking of God—is engendered by the illuminating work of the Spirit through the scriptural witness to the Son who calls and enables the church to know and respond in thankful praise to the Father for the gift of salvation.[12] As Robert Wall comments, "Wesley's sermons were centered by the grand themes of the *ordo salutis* and became theological commentaries on how God's salvation related to its audience in practical ways."[13]

Coming to know, trust, and love the Triune God in the present puts to rest fears about the need to prove the "contemporary relevance" of the Bible. Wesley's theological and pastoral wisdom illumines the need for congruence between knowing God's Word in Scripture and discerning God's work in the church, the kind of practical wisdom that constitutes good preaching.[14] As Wesley expressed this need:

Do I meditate therein day and night? Do I think (and consequently speak) thereof, "when I sit in the house, and when I walk by the way; when I lie down, and when I rise up?" By this means have I at length attained such a thorough knowledge as of the sacred text, so of its literal and spiritual meaning? Otherwise, how can I attempt to instruct others therein? Without this, I am a blind guide indeed! I am absolutely incapable of teaching my flock what I have never learned myself; no more fit to lead souls to God, than I am to govern the world.[15]

Much contemporary preaching tends to follow what was described by Hans Frei as the "great reversal," which has dominated the modern period.[16] This has become a matter of translating and fitting the biblical story into another world limited by that range of experience or reason open to anyone possessing "common sense," rather than incorporating that world into the scriptural narrative of the Triune God's dealings with creation, Israel, and the church. Frei's comments regarding eighteenth-century evangelical preaching are significant, especially with regard to Wesley:

> Such narrative sense as remained in the reading of the Bible found the connective narrative tissue which served as simultaneously as its own effective thread to present experience in the history of the soul's conversion and perfection . . . Wesley's . . . preaching testified with powerful eloquence to . . . belief in the redeeming death of Christ and its efficacy for the Christian. In other words, it is not a lack of appreciation for the importance of the occurrence character (the "objectivity") of crucial events which makes the piety of the evangelical awakening in England something other than realistic. They are objective and objectively transforming events, though the crucial evidence by which they become religiously certain is not external but internal to the soul. (Christ is not reduced, as people often claim about early Methodism, to a subjective experience). . . . The crucial and indispensable continuity or linkage in the story is the journey of the Christian person from sin through justification to sanctification or perfection. . . . Though real in his own right, the atoning Redeemer is at the same time a figure or type of the Christian's journey; for this is the narrative framework, the meaningful pattern within which alone the occurrence of the cross finds its applicative sense.[17]

Jason Vickers also argues that post-Reformation theology in England was marked by increasing distance between the Trinity, scriptural interpretation, and the Christian life due to a separation of theological reflection on the being of God from consideration of the work of God. His discusssion points toward recovery of a traditional understanding of the Trinity as the personal name of God—the "Father, Son, and Holy Spirit"—and its accompanying identifying descriptions of God's economy of creation and salvation. Of particular importance is Vickers's documentation of the shift in English Protestantism by which the church's rule of faith increasingly referred to Scripture rather than personal trust in and appropriate response to God and God's saving activity in Christ and the Holy Spirit. In other words, for much of the church's history salvation was not limited to intellectual assent to doctrinal propositions contained in Scripture, an epistemological concern with how we know and with proving what can be known. Rather, salvation was constituted by coming to know, trust, and love the Triune God in and through the sacramental practices of the church, or the means of grace, in an ontological and doxological way of knowing which is participatory and transformative.[18]

Vickers calls attention to the role played by the Wesleys in recovering the trinitarian name in hymns, prayers, and sermons, a vital reminder of the rightful home of trinitarian discourse in the worshiping life of the church and its true end of knowing, loving, and enjoying God. In other words, the Trinity, Scripture, the rule of faith, and salvation were integrally related in the church's work of worship, preaching, evangelism, and catechesis. As Vickers shows, this was similar to the understanding of the rule of faith in the early church, as summary identifying descriptions of the God whom Christians encountered in baptism and the Eucharist, and in prayer, praise, and preaching.[19]

Robert Cushman similarly observes that Wesley's "rule of faith," or practical divinity, maps a doctrinal way of salvation that is best summarized by the title of Wesley's sermon "The Scripture Way of Salvation." Grounded in the preaching of the gospel, this rule unfolds in the common affirmation of the church to its public expression in a common mind and verbal consent. In addition, as a confession of faith, the rule plays a regularized role in advancing the way of salvation as a disciplined process of redemption that is manifested in continual transformation of human existence into holiness of heart and life: "doctrine comes to life, the creed is made incarnate, and humanity participates in the divine nature."[20]

The comments by Vickers and Cushman are consistent with comments by Albert Outler, which also deserve our attention: "It seems clear that Wesley's conception of the *ordo salutis* is deeply influenced by Irenean doctrine," and "His [Wesley's] basic idea of the 'order of salvation'—as the process of the restoration to the image of God is obviously an adaptation of St. Ireaneaus's doctrine of . . . the recapitulatory work of Christ as the ground of all salvation."[21] Outler is referring to Irenaeus, second-century Bishop of Lyon, who was a salutary exemplar of classical Bible reading according to the rule of faith, the interpretation of Scripture as a single, unified, coherent narrative that witnesses to the God of Jesus Christ within the baptismal, eucharistic, and kerygmatic patterns of the church's liturgical life.

Arguably the first great postbiblical theologian of the church, Irenaeus summarized the apostolic witness to Triune God by means of a rule of faith or truth that identifies the one Creator who rules heaven and earth and is worshiped by the church, guides its interpretation of Scripture, informs the content of its preaching, and shapes its imagination and life.[22] Rowan Greer observes that Irenaeus was the first witness to a Christian Bible and a framework for its interpretation.

> The church came to insist that the God of Israel was the God of Jesus Christ and also that the significance of the Hebrew Scriptures lay in the testimony they bore to Christ. . . . For Christians, the dialogue between God and his people found its fullest expression in Christ, and so Christ became the key to the whole of Scripture. The theological and even christological convictions that determined how a Christian Bible was to be constituted then became central in shaping the interpretation of that Bible.[23]

For Irenaeus, the church's theology begins with the gracious movement of the Triune God toward creation and humanity. This personal knowledge is received and transmitted in the church's worship and practice, its prayers and catechesis, and the words, images, and stories of the biblical narrative. Thus the fundamental source of the vision or knowledge of God's glory revealed in Christ crucified and raised from the dead was what was accomplished and experienced in the prayer and praise of the church.

Liturgy and theology were intimately related by the new reality entrusted to and experienced by the apostles; the continued presence of the crucified and risen Lord was received and extended in assemblies that followed the Lord's command to baptize and to celebrate a supper of bread and wine in remembrance of him:

Baptism and Eucharist—it is the Lord's command that makes this a *lex orandi* (law of prayer). On the foundation of what God the Trinity accomplishes in these celebrations, and from the communities' experience of them, there developed a history of thought, a history of theology. Some ways of understanding things eventually became normative themselves: a *lex credendi* (law of believing).[24]

The liturgy, therefore, gave rise to both the interpretive framework and interpretation of the Christian Bible, the apostolic witness to the gospel of Jesus Christ through the medium of Scripture according to the pattern of the *regula fidei* or "rule of faith."[25]

For Irenaeus, then, Christian prayer, the sacraments, Scripture, preaching, virtue and devotion were all congruent with a trinitarian rule of faith.[26] The rule or canon for understanding and measuring the scriptural pattern of God's truth is most positively set forth by Irenaeus in a catechetical handbook, *The Proof or Demonstration of the Apostolic Preaching*, that provides a "summary memorandum" of Christian teaching, "the preaching of truth so as to strengthen your faith . . . to understand all the members of the body of truth . . . and receive the exposition of the things of God, so that . . . it will bear your own salvation like fruit."[27]

The *Demonstration* clearly and comprehensively unfolds the content of the Scriptures, the Old Testament, which points to the revelation of Jesus Christ as proclaimed by the apostles. Irenaeus thus sought to assist Christians in recognizing and following the scriptural authority of that preaching by demonstrating that the apostle's proclamation of what has been fulfilled in the death and resurrection of Christ, shaped as it is by Scripture, was indeed prophesied by the same God who created the world, elected Israel, and inspired the Law and the Prophets.[28] Because the true meaning of Scripture is theological, Irenaeus begins by confessing the Triune God, the source of Christian faith, hope and love.

> We must keep the rule (canon of faith) unswervingly, and perform the commandments of God, believing in God and fearing him; for he is the Lord, and loving Him . . . Faith exhorts us to remember that we have received baptism for the remission of sins, in the name of God the Father and in the name of Jesus

Christ, the Son of God, who was incarnate, and died, and was raised, and in the Holy Spirit of God, and that this baptism is the seal of eternal life and rebirth to God" (Dem. 3).

Irenaeus' confession of the Triune name leads to a reading of Ephesians 4:6 that illumines his liturgical and theological vision of Scripture: "One God and Father, who is above all and with all and in us all." This enabled Irenaeus to affirm that everything is created by the Father through his Word, while the Holy Spirit who is received in baptism enables us to cry, "Abba, Father," and forms us to the likeness of God (Dem. 5). Irenaeus' great theological accomplishment was the assertion of concrete, material conclusions—regarding the truth of God and humanity—drawn from the whole economy of God. In its trinitarian dimensions, the economy extends from the creation of all things to the creative work of the Spirit in baptism and moves to anticipating Christ's return in glory to consummate the peace and righteousness of God on earth.[29]

According to Irenaeus, these three articles—God the Father, the Son Christ Jesus, and the Holy Spirit—are the order of Christian faith and life and connected intimately to what happens in the liturgical experience of the church (Dem. 7).[30] This is summed up in a story expressing the continuity of Adam and Christ and of creation and redemption, one all-encompassing divine economy or history, embodied in Scripture, the rule of faith, and that finds its fullness in the new humanity of the incarnate Word.[31]

And this is the order of our faith, the foundation of the edifice and the support of our conduct: God, the Father, uncreated, uncontainable, invisible, one God, the Creator of all: this the first article of our faith. And the second article: The Word of God, the Son of God, Christ Jesus our Lord, who was revealed by the prophets according to the character of their prophecy and according to the nature of the economies of the Father, by whom all things were made, and who, in the last time, to recapitulate all things, became a man amongst men, visible and palpable, in order to abolish death, to demonstrate life, and to effect communion between God and man. And the third article: The Holy Spirit, through whom the prophets prophesied and the patriarchs learnt the things of God and the righteous were led in the path of righteousness, and who, in the last times, was poured out in a new fashion upon the human race renewing man, throughout the world, to God. (Dem. 6)

Of critical importance for Irenaeus is that the one God who is Creator and Redeemer of all things is known in the church's liturgy. In the saving activity of the Trinity those who bear the Spirit are led to the Son and the Son presents them to the Father: salvation is communion with God (Dem. 7). The liturgical knowledge of the Trinity as given and received in baptism provides the key or rule for understanding the whole Bible. Robert Wilken concludes, "The rule of faith had a Trinitarian structure whose narrative identified God by the things recorded in the Scriptures, the creation of the world, the inspiration of the prophets, the coming of Christ in the flesh, and the outpouring of the Holy Spirit. . . . The Bible is thus oriented toward a future still unfolding."[32]

Irenaeus' ruled way of reading Scripture was communal, ecclesial, and structured according to the trinitarian baptismal formula. The *regula fidei*, or rule of truth, served the church's hope of articulating and authenticating a world-encompassing story of the Triune God whose purpose—the fulfillment of all things in Jesus Christ—is revealed in creation, incarnation, redemption, and consummation: the hypothesis or plan of Scripture.[33] Scripture, then, intends to disclose the truth of God, the world, and human destiny by speaking of the one Jesus Christ, the manifestation of God's purpose for the whole creation as proclaimed by the apostles.

Moreover, the rule of faith is necessary for discerning the arrangement or economy of Scripture that renders the apostle's witness to the incarnate Lord who was announced by the Spirit in the Law and the Prophets. Christ himself is the purpose of the narrative and its exegesis; thus the scriptural texture of the apostolic preaching, the gospel proclaimed in the "wisdom of the Cross," is given voice within the whole canon; the God of Jesus Christ remains the subject and scope of Scripture that speaks of him in the Word, the incarnate form of salvation.[34]

The church, dispersed throughout the world to the ends of the earth, received from the apostles and their disciples the faith in one God the Father Almighty, "who made heaven and earth and sea and all that is in them (Ex. 20:11, and in one Jesus Christ, the Son of God, the incarnate for our salvation, and in the Holy Spirit, who through the prophets predicted the dispensations of God: the coming, the birth from the Virgin, the passion, the resurrection from the dead, and the ascension of the beloved Jesus Christ our Lord in the flesh into the heavens, and is coming from the heavens in the glory of the Father to "recapitulate all things" (Eph. 1:10) and raise up all flesh of the human race, so that to Christ Jesus our Lord and God and Savior and King, according to the good pleasure of the invisible Father, "every knee should bow, of beings in heaven and on earth and under the earth, and that every tongue should confess him." (AH, 1.10.1)

The relationship between Scripture, the gospel, doctrine, and the life and mission of the church in history is established in the proclamation of the whole narrative movement to its climax in cross and resurrection. Irenaeus described this as the "recapitulation of all things," a summary or restatement that provides a way of seeing the person of Christ, the incarnate Word who defeated the power of sin and overcame death to accomplish the purpose of God revealed through the whole economy.[35] Moreover, the recapitulation of all things in Christ was essential for Irenaeus' theology since it united Christian content and form: Christ and creation, the Old Testament and Israel, the divinity of Christ and his humanity, Christian people and participation in Christ's ministry of self-giving, suffering, and death for the world. By thinking within the faith confessed by the church as revealed in the scriptural narrative and summarized in the apostles' preaching, Irenaeus affirmed that salvation is not from the world but occurs in and for its perfection, thus overcoming a dualism of the material and spiritual, or creation and redemption.[36]

The Incarnation represents the culminating economy of God: "The work of the Word in creation and in the Old Testament finds its completion when the Word is made flesh."[37] By attending to the whole narrative of Scripture, Irenaeus contemplated God's work in Christ as articulated in Ephesians 1:9–10, "For he has made known to us in all wisdom and insight the mystery of his will, according to his purpose which he set forth in Christ as a plan for the fullness of time to unite all things in him, things in heaven and things on earth." Paul Blowers observes, "The challenge of Christian identity was to reconstruct the story of Jesus Christ in its dramatic fullness as both the cosmic story—a narrative comprehending the destiny of all creation and all peoples—and as the genuine 'final act' to the peculiar sacred story of Israel."[38]

In its reading of Scripture as the revelation of God's dealings with the world, the church is invited to discover its life within that providential story to become itself a witness to God's purpose of uniting and perfecting the creation through the Son and the Spirit in divine glory.[39] Irenaeus' theological wisdom guided preachers to read each text of Scripture with the whole in mind and to locate each individual sermon text within the whole canon. Christian Scripture is a whole because it is the whole narrative of the one Triune God, and in order to follow the whole story preachers must know the whole story's plot and its characters. Moreover, since the church is a continuous community with the story's actors and narrators, it has no need to translate the message of the Bible to make it "relevant" for contemporary listeners, but must learn to see, or imagine, itself as one with God's people across time, as a single community created by the Spirit through the Word of God, which is its true witness.[40] Rowan Greer notes:

> From one point of view, the Rule of Faith was limited as a unifying framework for interpreting scripture. It did not settle the question of method, nor did it solve problems of detail in theological, moral, and spiritual exposition of the Bible. But from another point of view, what seem to be limitations are precisely what enable the task of interpretation. Built into the patristic vision of exegesis is the conviction that the Christian's theological vision continues to grow and change, just as the Christian life is a pilgrimage and progress toward a destiny only dimly perceived. The framework of interpretation, then, does not so much solve the problem of what scripture means as supply the context in which the quest for that meaning may take place.[41]

Irenaeus' theological and pastoral wisdom illumines significant challenges related to the interpretation of Scripture and proclamation of the gospel. For example, many preachers view the Bible as an ancient book that can be visited to find useful ideas, topics, and illustrations for explaining how Christianity might be made "contemporary," or functionally useful and relevant to listeners. However, such accommodationist strategies are incapable of inhabiting the world of Scripture according to the rule of faith in order to know its realities and speak its language as an expression of Christian wisdom; preaching that calls out and forms a holy people to embody the mission of the

Triune God in the world. Outler's assessment is significant for understanding the theological and soteriological orientation of Wesley's reading of Scripture for preaching: "It seems clear that Wesley's conception of the *ordo salutis* is deeply influenced by Irenean doctrine."

Becoming What We Read

Wesley's theological orientation points us toward the recovery of "good preaching" as a form of intelligent and passionate witness to the presence and work of the Triune God. Such testimony is narrated by the whole of Scripture and expressed through theological discourse that is characterized by the truth and goodness revealed in creation and fulfilled by Christ. Wesley urged members of the clergy to examine their devotion and desire for God according to the divine: human logic of the Incarnation.

> Am I . . . such as I ought to be, with regard to my affections? I am taken from among and ordained for men, in things pertaining to God. I stand between God and man, by the authority of the great Mediator, in the nearest and most endearing relation both to my Creator and fellow creatures. Have I accordingly given my heart to God, and to my brethren for his sake? Do I love God with all my soul and strength, and my neighbor, every man, as myself? Does this love swallow me up, possess me whole, constitute my supreme happiness? Does it animate my tempers and passions, and regulate all my powers and faculties? Is it the spring which gives rise to all my thoughts, and governs all my words and actions.[42]

Wesley described mere assent to theological opinions, or "dead" orthodoxy, as the antithesis of true or "living faith" that is awakened by the Spirit through the witness of Scripture to the Father's self-giving in Christ. In addition, he held that "the ever blessed Trinity" is one of the essential doctrines contained in the "oracles of God"—Holy Scripture—and interwoven with "living faith" that God bestows in order to be known and loved by us.[43]

> But I know not how anyone can be a Christian believer till "he hath" (as St. John speaks) "the witness in himself," "till the Spirit of God witnesses with his Spirit that he is a child of God—that is, in effect, till God the Holy Ghost witnesses that God the Father has accepted him through the merits of God the Son—and having this witness he honours the Son and blessed Spirit "even as he honours the Father."[44]

Wesley's preaching gives homiletic expression to the knowledge of faith that works through love within a tradition of shared beliefs and practices that was guided by the faith expressed in the creeds. In other words, the truth and goodness by which the Spirit orders the intellect and will to the fellowship of the Father and the Son is a necessary presupposition for preaching as an expression of "Scriptural Christianity." Wainwright comments on Wesley's Trinitarian hermeneutics:

> Study of the Scriptures in the Spirit, by whom they were divinely written, conveys the incarnate Christ, who gives knowledge of the Father who sent him, so that we may love Him and thus be conformed to the Son and enjoy the holiness which the Spirit gives.[45]

For Wesley, reading Scripture is guided by a conviction that the truth and reality of the Triune God is mediated by the testimony of the Spirit to Christ through the whole biblical canon; a participatory and transformative way of reading that includes but also exceeds the historical, cultural, and linguistic matters related to the biblical text. In other words, Wesley's theological orientation does not exclude the historical and human dimensions of study, ministry, and preaching but rather seeks their completion in God.[46]

For example, in "An Address to the Clergy" Wesley counsels ministers to become persons of sound learning, piety, and virtue. He identifies the need for acquiring the capacities of understanding, apprehension, judgment, and reason in relation to a number of subjects: knowledge of the world and of human nature, character, dispositions and tempers; knowledge of the sciences, natural history, metaphysics, and philosophy; competence in thinking logically and speaking clearly; and possessing the virtue of courage for speaking the truth in love. To these he adds serious engagement with the Fathers of the Church, especially their interpretation of Scripture. Wesley gives strongest emphasis to knowing Scripture, which will entail critical mastery of its original languages, its grammar and genres, as well as a grasp of its parts in relation to the whole—the analogy of faith—as the clue for unfolding its literal and spiritual senses for listeners. At the same time, only the wisdom of God the Divine Teacher is sufficient for bringing to completion these intellectual pursuits and tasks.

They [ministers] are assured of being assisted in all their labour by Him who teacheth man knowledge. And who teacheth like Him? Who, like Him, giveth wisdom to the simple? How easy is it for Him, (if we desire it, and believe that he is both able and willing to do this,) by the powerful, though secret, influences of the Spirit, to open and enlarge our understanding; to strengthen all our faculties; to bring to our remembrance whatsoever things are needful, and to fix and sharpen our attention to them; so that we may profit above all who wholly depend upon themselves, in whatever may qualify us for our Master's work.[47]

This participatory way of knowing is evoked by God's self-gift in Christ and appropriated into human life through the Spirit's gifts, empowerments, and fruit. A historical interpretation can only be preparatory for this, while a Christian reading of Scripture is oriented toward the living Christ revealed through the words of the Bible, toward what Scripture means for the lives of Christians and what it promises for the future of the church and the world. For theological reasons, a "grammar of participation" provides a more fitting alternative to a "grammar of representation": [those] "modern and early modern tendencies toward skills of negotiating new products, new texts, and introduction of new technologies for organizing words and related *techne*, or craft, for realizing these texts."[48]

This description of "representation" sheds light on assumptions that continue to influence modern homiletic practice and the other theological disciplines. In the case of preaching, for example, a "grammar of representation" is related closely to a "technology of Scripture," or the "freezing of words" on the written page of "the text," which has increasingly appeared on PowerPoint presentations and other popular forms of "messaging." On either the book or screen, however, the "freezing of words" privileges mathematical accuracy and universal methods for arranging and transmitting knowledge, "[instantiating] new dualisms, between reader and text, form and content, subject and object . . . and which [end] in Enlightenment deistic and theistic discourse."[49]

Such popular dualisms contribute to the "hypostatization" of sermons—the literalization of discrete words and ideas abstracted from Scripture as "text"—but that preclude participation in the saving activity of Christ through the presence and work of the Spirit. In other words, when the practice of preaching is defined by a technical, theologically neutral process divorced from its ecclesial and liturgical home, its discourse will tend toward abstract, a-temporal, timeless "words about words" that "stand for" something else: that is, an event in the distance past, a "meaning" or "principle" behind the text, an idea or feeling within the individual hearer, the preacher's favorite agenda or program.

Wesley's homiletic theology is grounded in and expressive of a way of reading Scripture that is participatory, "in accord with the Christian and biblical understanding of reality, [that] should envision history not only as a linear unfolding of individual moments, but also as an ongoing participation in God's active providence, both metaphysically and christologically-pneumatologically."[50] In other words, participating in the life of God as humans and members of Christ's body—through the work of Christ and the Spirit—gathers up past, present, and future realities into a unified whole. The distance between Scripture and the present is not a mere historical or cultural gap that can be overcome by making the Bible "relevant" through translating its message into a contemporary idiom. There is also spiritual and moral distance between Scripture and the present that is overcome only by the work of the Spirit that engenders repentance, conversion, and the power to live a transformed life by faith in Christ. In the classical tradition, then, this vision included the assumption that the context of biblical interpretation was provided by the church, creeds, and doctrine, as well as worship, preaching, and sacraments.[51]

The aim of interpretation and preaching is to seek and to proclaim the presence of the divine realities to which the whole canon of Scripture leads. This does not preclude historical, linguistic, or literary ways of reading, but recognizes that God's creative and redemptive work is both linear and participatory, and will, as such, be illumined by doctrinal judgments that turn our attention to God. Levering brings to light the fact that participatory exegesis is capable of accounting for divine and human dimensions in accord with the logic of the Incarnation, but without bringing them into competition, since God is both the source and goal of human knowledge, desire, action, and speech.[52]

In the preface to the 1746 *Sermons on Several Occasions*, Wesley offers insight on the nature of the "plain truth" that constitutes his preaching:

To candid reasonable men I am not afraid to lay open what have been the inmost thoughts of my heart. I have though, I am a creature of the day, passing through life as an arrow through the air. I am a spirit come from God and return ing to God; just hovering over the great gulf, till a few moments hence I am no more seen; I drop into an unchangeable eternity. I want to know one thing, the way to heaven—how to land safe on that happy shore. God himself has conde scended to teach the way; for this very end he came from heaven. He hath writ ten it down in a book. O give me that book! At any price give me the Book of God![53]

Wesley's theological orientation is concerned with reading Scripture in light of the work of the One God who creates us and redeems us. Acknowledging those readers whose understanding of the world, human life, and God is attained by the light of reason, he describes himself as a creature of the day whose existence is fleeting and passing quickly. Citing the both classical and Christian sources, he acknowledges humanity's finitude and desire for immor tality, affirming we are from God and long to return to God, suspended over a "great gulf" until we cease to exist and pass into eternity.[54] Moving from a description of creaturely existence and immortal longing to the truths of divine revelation, Wesley voices a desire to know the way to heaven, for per sonal, intimate knowledge of God that is dependent upon holiness, or the illu minating presence of the Holy Spirit.

Wesley asserts God himself has condescended to teach this way: the saving purpose for which he "came down from heaven." This way is written down in the book of Holy Scripture, which is the "book of God."[55] Wesley's preface provides a brief metaphysical and theological orientation to his expression of the central truths of Scripture in his sermons. Because of the Incarnation, the language of Scripture and preaching is capable of referring to more than just ourselves and our context. Levering comments:

This is so because exegesis . . . that participates doctrinally and spiritually in the realities depicted by Scripture, and thus reading Scripture not merely as a record of something strictly in the past, requires a sense that all human time partici pates metaphysically (order of creation) and Christologically and pneumatolog ically (order of grace) in God's eternal providence, and therefore that not historical text can be studied strictly on its own terms. History matters, but in a participatory relation to the creative and redemptive work of the Son and the Spirit that enable Christians to become partakers of the divine nature through the verbal witness of Scripture.[56]

Wesley's sermons attempt to set forth the wisdom of Jesus Christ that illumines the proper relation between God and human creatures, or knowledge of reality. Although some knowledge of God and ourselves is available through creation, this is to be measured theologically, in light of God's teaching in the incarnate Word who "came down from heaven," to become our way of returning to God. In addition, the way taught by Christ is intrinsically related to its source and end, embracing past, present, and future. Wesley's comments to "reasonable" men are illumined by the light of the Person of Christ, fully divine and fully human, through whom human creatures have been created and redeemed to participate in God's life. In other words, the "more" human creatures desire is found in the mind of Christ, human reason informed by the gifts of faith and love. Moreover, this relationship is revealed by God in the Incarnation, the doctrinal confession enfleshed and enacted by the church according to the "book of God." Stephen Long writes:

> In Christian theology, the incarnation is where God's eternity and creation's temporality meet. What is the relationship between God and creation? Any answer to this question must be given in Christological terms. In fact, Christians claim the answer is given before we even know how to ask the proper question. . . . Because the incarnation provides the answer for the question as to how God and creation relate, it also provides the answer for how we must think about the relationship between faith and reason.[57]

The restoration of humanity to the divine image requires a trinitarian reading of Scripture for its intelligibility. Wesley demonstrates this in the sermon the "Scripture Way of Salvation" by uniting creation and redemption, beginning with prevenient grace, the light that leads to repentance and an acknowledgment of the need for divine grace.

> All the drawings of the "Father, the desires after God, if we yield to them increase more and more; all that 'light' wherewith the Son of God 'enlighteneth everyone that cometh into the world' showing every man 'to do justly, to love

mercy, and to walk humbly with his God;' all convictions which his Spirit from time to time works in every child of man, it is true, the generalities of men stifle them as soon as possible, and after a while, forget, or at least deny, that they had them."[58]

Having affirmed the participation of humanity in the mind of the Triune Creator, Wesley discusses redemption in light of justifying and sanctifying grace. Through the work of Christ and the Spirit we are made to participate in our restoration to God's image; the renewal of our humanity in the holy love that God originally intended.

> We are inwardly changed by the power of God. We feel the love of God shed abroad in our hearts by the Holy Ghost which is given unto us, producing love to all mankind, and more especially to the children of God; expelling the love of the world, the love of pleasure, of ease, of honour, of money; with pride, anger, self-will, and every other evil temper—in a word changing the earthly, sensual, devlish, mind into "the mind that was in Christ Jesus."[59]

Learning to read Scripture according to the "analogy of faith" engenders preaching that participates in the incarnate Wisdom who is the purpose of creation and redemption. In other words, Wesley's reading of Scripture was articulated in preaching that was both reasonable and doctrinally regulated. The message of preaching—"Scriptural holiness"—is also the medium of preaching. For this reason, there needs to be congruence between what is preached and the life of those who preach and those who hear: the restoration of humanity to the image of God that transforms us from original sin through repentance, justification, and the new birth to entire sanctification.[60] As Wesley happily describes the "analogy of faith":

> There is a wonderful analogy between all these; and a close and intimate connexion between the chief heads of that faith "which was once delivered to the saints." Every article, therefore, concerning which there is any question should be determined by this rule; every doubtful scripture interpreted according to the grand truths which run through the whole.[61]

Outler observes that Wesley regarded the *Preface to the Sermons on Several Occasions* as definitive for his entire project of sermon publication, "the aim here is to set the mood for a mutual understanding between the evangelist and his readers, a point of reference for their interpretations of his "doctrine, rhetoric, and spirit."[62] This practical wisdom was the fruit of indwelling the world of Scripture that illumines our minds for seeing the world rightly, thereby bearing witness to the work of the Father through the Son and in the Spirit who creates and restores humanity to share the divine image.

Prayerful study, faithful obedience, and the wisdom of love were the means by which Wesley sought to know and understand the things of God and the way to God: "I lift up my heart to the Father of lights," intending to obey what God speaks, "If any be willing to do thy will, he shall know." Open to the prompting and leading of the Spirit, Wesley immersed himself in the whole of Scripture, "with all the attention and earnestness of which my mind is capable." Pursuing a truth that exceeds human understanding and desire, he conversed with "those experienced in the things of God, and then the writings thereby, being dead, they yet speak." Attentive to the teaching of Scripture, the wisdom of the Christian past, and the illuminating work of the Spirit, Wesley prepared himself for proclaiming the "way to heaven," by "faith that works through love."[63] The truth of God matters in preaching.

CHAPTER 6

THE SPREAD OF VIRTUE
AND HAPPINESS

Methodism is the old religion, the religion of the Bible, the religion of the
Primitive Church, the religion of the Church of England. This old religion . . .
is not other than love, the love of God and of all mankind. . . . This love is the
great medicine of life. . . . Wherever this is, there are virtue and happiness going
hand in hand. . . . This religion of love and joy and peace has its seat in the
inmost soul; but is ever showing itself by its fruits . . . spreading virtue and happiness to all around it.[1]

Wesley offered these reflections as he neared the end of many
years of preaching and ministry. I am particularly interested in
his description of Methodism as the old religion of the heart—
love, joy, and peace—and its fruit—"spreading virtue and happiness"—in
relation to the practice of preaching. His assessment of the healing power
of the religion of love lends a distinctive spiritual and moral character to
the life and mission of Methodism that warrants our attention. My aim in
this chapter, then, is to explore the practical wisdom of Wesley's commitment to the religion holiness and happiness in conversation with the work
of two other preachers and teachers of preachers, Augustine and Thomas
Aquinas.

Albert Outler argues that while Wesley adhered to the Reformation doctrine
of justification through God's work in Christ, he also discovered the doctrine of
holiness—of heart and life—as the true agenda and final good of both creaturely and Christian existence. He was thereby able to integrate evangelical and
catholic sensibilities, a theology of the cross with a theology of glory, giving his
doctrine of the Christian life a particular richness. Wesley's vision emphasizes
the mysterious interaction of God and human creatures in redemption, our participation in "working out our salvation with fear and trembling" through living

faith and its manifestations, which was encapsulated on numerous occasions in sermons as "holiness and happiness."[2]

Wesley, in other words, was a teleological thinker, which means he understood that all our truly human aspirations are oriented toward happiness; and that this relentless human hunger for happiness can only be satisfied by sharing and being conformed to God's holiness.[3] For this reason, the aim of Methodists in their preaching, teaching, and practicing of "Bible religion" was the spread of virtue and happiness which essence is love; the perfect love of God and neighbor ruling over, in, and through all other loves, desires, and intentions. This means that preaching itself can be an act of moral happiness: the joy of knowing and speaking the Word according to the new law of the gospel through the presence and work of Christ and the Holy Spirit.

A few selections from Wesley's sermons will help to demonstrate the importance of this emphasis. For example, in the sermon "The Way to the Kingdom," which was first preached in 1742, Wesley describes the religion of the heart, stating it consists of neither right theological opinions, forms, and ceremonies, nor morality. While these are necessary, they are not sufficient.

> The Apostle sums it all up in three particulars: "righteousness, and peace, and joy in the Holy Ghost" . . . Thou shalt love the Lord thy God with all thy heart and with all thy mind, and with all thy soul, and with all thy strength. This is the first and great commandment, the first great branch of Christian righteousness. Thou shalt delight thyself in the Lord thy God; thou shalt seek and find all happiness in him.

At the same time, such love for God implies love for the neighbor, and seeks that happiness in God and for the love of God, "thou shalt love thy neighbor as thyself, in being lovers of all humanity, doing good to all, full of mercy and good works." Wesley then adds, "But true religion, or a right heart toward God and man, implies happiness as well as holiness. For it is not only righteousness—fulfilling the law through faith—but also peace and joy in the Holy Ghost."[4]

Peace with God is joy in the Holy Spirit of God. This is important for its emphasis on the life of God indwelling that engenders enjoyment of God's reconciling work in Christ, "Blessed (or rather, happy . . .) is the man whose unrighteousness is forgiven, and whose sin is forgiven." The Holy Spirit inspires such joy and happiness through faith in God's favor, filling us with hope of participating in God's final glory through the restoration of our lives in God's image. Wesley concludes, "This holiness and happiness, joined in one, are sometimes syted in the inspired writings, 'the Kingdom of God' because it is the immediate fruit of God's reigning in the soul."[5]

In a sermon dated 1740, "The Righteousness of Faith," Wesley contrasts the faith of the law and the righteousness of faith. The law, which was given to Adam and Eve in paradise, required obedience as the condition of remaining in the holiness and happiness in which they were created, a continuance of God's favor and God's knowledge and love. On the other hand, the righteousness that is of faith is given to those who are "unholy and unhappy," and having fallen short of God's glory know the wrath of God, the power of sin, and the effects of spiritual, moral, and physical death. The covenant of grace, or the righteousness of faith, is given in order to recover our favor and life in God. This is the wisdom of God that reveals God's goodness. Wesley concludes with this insight:

> It is wisdom to aim at the best end by the best means. Now the best end which any creature can pursue is happiness in God. And the best end a fallen creature can pursue is the recovery of the favor and image of God, which is better than life itself. And this is by the righteousness of faith, believing in the only-begotten Son of God.[6]

For Wesley, holiness and happiness are correlates that are constituted by knowing and loving God, an enjoyment that is life itself. He articulated this truth in trinitarian form in one of his earliest sermons, "The Circumcision of the Heart":

> The one perfect good shall be your ultimate end. On thing shall ye desire for its own sake—the fruition of him that is all in all. One happiness shall you propose to your souls, even an union with him that made them, the having fellowship with the Father and the Son, the being joined to the "Lord in one Spirit." One design ye are to pursue to the end of time—the enjoyment of God in time and eternity—desire other things so far as they tend to this. Love the creature—as it leads to the Creator. But in every step you take be it this glorious point that

terminates your view. Let every affection, and thought, and word, and work be subordinate to this. Whatever ye desire or fear, whatever ye seek or shun, whatever ye think, speak, or do, be it in order to your happiness in God, the sole end as well as the source of your being.[7]

The true happiness for which human creatures longs is found in knowing and loving God, the gift that God the Father is pleased to give through the truth and goodness made known in the Son, which is realized by the work of the Holy Spirit. In a sermon during the latter years of his ministry, "Spiritual Worship," Wesley writes that it is

> then that happiness begins—happiness real, solid, substantial. . . . Then it is that heaven is opened in the soul, that the proper heavenly state commences, while the love of God, as loving us, is shed abroad in the heart, instantly producing love to all mankind: general, pure, benevolence, together with its genuine fruits, lowliness, meekness, patience, contentedness in every state; an entire clear, full acquiescence in the whole will of God, enabling us to rejoice evermore, and in everything to give thanks.[8]

Wesley concludes that when we dwell in Christ and Christ dwells in us we are happy, since the Creator/human creature is restored to the truth and love revealed in the Incarnation. Echoing Augustine, Wesley states, "This one God made our heart from himself; and it cannot rest till it resteth in him." Wesley contrasts happiness in God with other forms of happiness, including youthfulness, physical vigor and health, fortune, convenience, and an abundance of things. Because natural blessings are fleeting and like shadows, they are neither solid nor substantive enough to give permanent satisfaction. To make this point Wesley cites Homer, "Amidst our plenty something still to me, to thee, to him is wanting," and then adds, "That something is neither more not less than the knowledge and love of God—without which no spirit can be happy in either heaven and earth."[9]

Happiness in God

Augustine was no stranger to the joy of coming to know and love God by faith in Christ through the ministry and fellowship of the church. Through an extended process of repentance, confession, and forgiveness his mind was changed to see that human love and desire, the restlessness that seeks certitude and control through attachment to created things, will only be satisfied when drawn to share in the happiness of the Triune God. Our life is doxological, in that we are made good and happy through the offering of ourselves as acts of praise and thanksgiving to the Father in union with Christ. As Augustine writes in *Confessions*: "You have made us for yourself, and our heart is restless until it rests in you" (Confessions, I.I). Christopher Thompson comments:

> The normative guiding principle guiding the *Confessions* is the doctrine of the Church concerning God as the Triune Creator of all that exists and Redeemer of all who seek reconciliation . . . the overriding motif of any narrative of Christian experience is the claim that "God has made us for himself." . . . This is the drama of the revelatory narratives: that I find in them, not confirmation of myself, but every constitution of myself. I do not place the actions of God within the horizon of my story; rather, I place my story within the action of God.[10]

Augustine's new identity was constituted by a new narrative in which the disparate worlds of God and humanity were happily made one in the economy of salvation that finds its center in Christ and its enactment in the life of the church. Not of Augustine's making, this new world was the gift and work of divine love engendering a new language and way of life through faith in the Incarnation, the Word made flesh. This is the way of happiness that consists of knowing and loving God, and that transforms us to see the world in light of the Wisdom mediated by Christ through the witness of Scripture.[11]

Early Christian ethics took root in the soil of ancient moral philosophy; imitation, the virtues, interior dispositions, character and transformation into the divine image and likeness. This tradition was not rejected, rather its framework was maintained, adapted, and altered to fit God's self-revelation in Christ. Moreover, the Sermon on the Mount provided the call to be holy, to be "perfect as your Father in heaven is perfect." Christians understood their life in light of this larger end, a teleological ordering of human life inherited from ancient wisdom that was reoriented by the eschatological fulfillment of God's good purposes in the ministry of Christ. Human actions were therefore assessed and judged when directed to the most praiseworthy of all ends, the

Triune God who is the supreme good, a good, however, which is not itself a means to other ends.[12]

The aim of this vision was to lead people to living a happy life in God in accord with the truest and deepest aspirations of humanity. It was significant, then, that the Beatitudes begin with "blessed" or "happy," so that Jesus is heard as the Teacher of Wisdom who himself is the Way to happiness that is the goal of human life. The Beatitudes were therefore read as depicting both the character of true happiness and the way leading to that goal. God is the highest good, since nothing else is sufficient for human creatures made in God's image, so that the end hoped for was also present in the beginning. Communion with God, consisting of knowledge, love, and delight, brings fulfillment to human life; only our return to God by grace and for communion brings genuine human happiness. As Robert Wilken observes, for the early Christians holy and happiness were one:

> For Christians, the moral life and the religious life were complimentary. Although thinking about the moral life moved within a conceptual framework inherited from Greek and Latin moralists, Christian thinkers redefined the good by making fellowship with the living God the end; revised the beginning by introducing the teaching that we are made in the image of God, and complicating the middle with talk of the intractability and inevitability of sin.[13]

Christian virtue and happiness were seen as the "more" human creatures desired, longed for, and which is known and received through the activity of God. Moreover, because the Christian life is trinitarian, Christian virtue and happiness are possessed in Christ and bestowed by the Holy Spirit.

Augustine set forth this message of beatitude or happiness in his exposition of the Sermon on the Mount as the perfect rule or pattern of Christian life. Augustine read the Beatitudes of Jesus as addressing the deep, human hunger for truth and goodness. The way of happiness leads to wisdom, peace, and God's will, satisfying the whole of a human being in its restoration to the image of God. Following patristic wisdom, Augustine interpreted the new law taught by Jesus as the presence of the Holy Spirit in the human heart, just as it is the Spirit who inscribes the content of God's law on the tables of the heart. To emphasize the new reality made possible by Christ, Augustine joined the Beatitudes with the gifts of the Spirit that accompany the Spirit's indwelling and sanctifying grace. These, in turn, were joined to the seven petitions of the Lord's Prayer.[14]

Augustine's exposition of the Sermon on the Mount articulates a vision of the Christian life ordered by Christ's blessings in Matthew 5, and the messianic gifts of the Holy Spirit as enumerated in Isaiah 11:2–3. Moreover, Augustine read the prayer of Jesus in Matthew 6 as the perfect prayer that sustains Christian people on this journey. Augustine's practical wisdom was influential in placing the New Law of the gospel and the Sermon on the Mount at the center of the Christian moral life. He saw the teaching of Jesus as addressing the human desire for happiness; attributing this to the authority of its Teacher whose Word is able to penetrate the depths of human hearts; responds to the deepest human aspirations; purifies the darkest of human desires; and reorders human thoughts, affections, and actions to God. In other words, coming to know and love the Teacher and his teaching is true wisdom. This wisdom is the fruit of desire for the truth that is inseparable from the virtues of faith, hope, and love, a life that shares in God's goodness and is happy, ordering all lesser ends in relation to God and the love of God.[15]

Augustine's teaching on the Beatitudes, virtues, and gifts was taken up and extended by Thomas Aquinas during the thirteenth century. Writing in the *Summa Theologiae*, Aquinas establishes that

> happiness as the end of human life as is evident from Augustine's words . . . the sermon, which Our Lord delivered on the mountain, contains the whole process of forming the life of the Christian. Therein men's interior movements are ordered. Because after declaring that his end is Beatitude; and after commending the teaching of the Gospel was to be promulgated, He orders man's interior movements, first in regard to man himself, secondly in regard to his neighbor.[16]

As a master preacher and teacher whose primary interest was the formation of preachers, the work of Thomas Aquinas unites prayerful study with faithful obedience for proclaiming the gospel through faith in Christ and the grace of the Holy Spirit.

In the *Summa Theologiae*, Aquinas unfolds the pattern of divine revelation—God creating, saving, and perfecting—with the first two parts being seen as an elaborate statement of the *dramatis personae*, God and humanity, with a supporting cast of other creatures.[17] This drama consists in the bringing together of God and us in beatitude, a happiness created by grace in loving communion with God. This drama centers on the Son, who is "the wisdom of the art of the Father," the model and objective foundation of our movement toward God. Thus the incarnate Word revealed in Jesus Christ is the Way by which we are restored to the divine image as well as its Truth.[18]

The work of A. N. Williams demonstrates the primary focus of the *Summa* is God, not "how" but "who," so that Thomas is most interested in setting forth a theology that contemplates the union of God and the human being created in God's image.[19] His aim is to render intelligible both who God is and who God has created us to be. In leading us to Christ, moreover, Aquinas leads us to see the One in whom that union has taken place because of who God is. This wisdom challenges dualistic notions separating the creator and human creatures, while presenting their proper roles and integrity from the perspective of God's intentions made inherent in us by the operation of divine grace enabling our human capacities ("Mystical Theology Redux," 56).

Williams notes that, for Thomas, God has destined us for a union with himself that lies beyond our grasp; since to approach God is only possible through God and not by any other means. We are human creatures who, in creation, have come from God's eternal happiness in his Triune being, and who, in redemption, are returning to the Triune God as our eternal happiness with the blessed in heaven. Our salvation as human creatures, the flourishing of our humanity, is found in neither ourselves nor the things of creation, but is in being drawn to God in a union that begins imperfectly in this life and will be perfected in the next. And this is all of divine grace, God's own self-giving, so that the joy it creates is none other than God himself and our participation in the divine goodness that God creates in us himself ("Mystical Theology Redux," 60–61).

For Thomas, then, in both this life and the next our fullest happiness and well-being as human creatures is attained through a transformation flowing from, and leading to, the joy of knowing and loving God. God is not useful for achieving human purposes, rather God is the One in whose relation our life is given as both a gift and means of sanctification in, through, and for Godself. The practices of prayerful study, loving devotion, and humble obedience transform and move us to live well in returning to God as the object of faith and satisfaction of the heart's desire, "the joy we associate with union with God, the bliss of paradise" ("Mystical Theology Redux," 60–61).

Everything in the *Summa*, including the communicative dimension of theology, must be seen in light of this end; the participation of graced human beings in the life of the blessed or happy in heaven. Study and prayer share the same goal and belong to the same charitable movement that overflows into an active life of teaching and preaching: "We do not speak in order that others might be persuaded; we speak because we have been transformed to know and love God through the union of our minds with the Triune God" ("Mystical Theology Redux," 69).

For Aquinas, participation in the liturgical and sacramental life of the church immerses us in the appropriate means by which we enter into and proceed in this movement. As the true teacher of the church, Christ is also the measure of its doctrine, giving himself to the whole community in its performance of the story of his life, death, and resurrection that calls it into being.[20] Thus the truth we believe, love, and obey is Christ himself indwelling the church through the Spirit's grace.

> The indwelling Christ give us a kind of instruction by which the intellect bursts out in love's affection, a taste of himself which is a "certain experiential knowledge," so that we might hold fast to what he says, to a truth we do not see. . . . In the end, it seems, that we believe the teaching of Scripture and creed not because reason gives us compelling grounds to do so, still less that we wish it merely were true, but because we have suffered the things of which it speaks.[21]

The *Summa* displays an integral but distinct relation between God and human creatures, dependent upon the knowledge and love of God for its intelligibility, and communicating the conviction that doctrine and life are inseparable within a framework of humanity's restoration to, and renewal in, the divine image. And while this unity is theological and intellectual, it is also ontological and dynamic, in that it attempts "to reproduce the very movement of wisdom and the divine action in the work of creation—culminating in [human creatures] the image of God—and in the work of divine government, which leads all creatures back to God their ultimate goal and happiness."[22] In being drawn to know the truth and love its goodness we are rendered conformable to Christ through the Spirit's grace, thus engendering the joy of intelligent, loving attention to the Word and communicating its fruits in preaching. Nicholas Healy writes of this joy,

> the Christian life can be one of great joy . . . since the acquisition of good habits disposes us to good actions, often making them a pleasure, and forgiveness is readily available. So we must delight in God for God's own sake, as being our last end, and in virtuous deeds, not as being our end, but for the sake of their inherent goodness which is delightful to the virtuous.[23]

Fergus Kerr comments on this matter of happiness as the true end of human life, a kind of "practical theology" situated by Aquinas between the mysteries of faith: the joy of participating in the Triune life through the wisdom incarnate in the Word and the Spirit's gift of charity that establishes loving friendship with God.

> In effect he [Aquinas] sought to develop an ethos based not on obedience to this or that divine command, but in terms of the formation of the kind of person who appropriates and develops the gifts required for a moral life in view of the promised enjoyment of divine beatitude, a sovereign bliss which is God's own life. His interest is not in the rules we have to follow but in the kind of people we become, as we practice this or that virtue or vice—of course in accordance with this or that expression of the divine law but principally in accomplishing the good which alone is our ultimate happiness.[24]

Aquinas communicates a vision of God who has made human creatures for himself, constituting us in such a way that we will never be satisfied, or happy, except in the measure that we more and more deeply resemble the divine image as our truest end. God has placed a desire in us to return to him; our final and perfect beatitude will only consist in the vision of the divine essence, and we will not be perfectly happy as long as there remains something of God to desire and seek. The whole of human life—intellectually, emotionally, and bodily—unfolds in desiring, embracing, and enjoying God as the source and goal of all human knowing and loving, the transformation of our human capacities that leads to the divine image restored and our final end attained.[25] Or as Nicholas Lash states, "God is the object of our faith as the heart's desire, as goal towards which all our life and thought is set."[26]

The origin of all this is the Triune God who communicates his goodness with human persons who have been created to share his image. The means of this communication is a participation in the Son through the grace of the Spirit whose power engenders a new nature in Christ and new way of living characterized principally by charity. This end orients the moral life of Christians, and is the end of human beings, the work of sanctification that has its primary source in the grace of Christ, who is both Son of God and truly human like us.

According to Aquinas, the happiness for which we are created to share is unattainable through external goods, possessions, or riches, either natural or made, since these are destined to serve human creatures rather than rule them. Neither can human honors obtain the fullness of happiness, nor human fame, glory, or power. Aquinas excludes these as external ends along with the goals of life, health, and pleasure, indentifying them as goods that are to be enjoyed in seeking our final good in God.[27]

Only the happiness enjoyed by the Triune God is perfect and good, and therefore capable of entirely satisfying human desire. The object of the human will is the universal good; while the object of the human intellect is universal truth; God alone is capable of satisfying human minds and hearts by communicating himself as perfect Truth and Goodness. For this reason, the person who desires to embrace a life of Christian virtue will live happily according to the truth and goodness by which God has accomplished the salvation of humanity through the Incarnation and outpouring of the Holy Spirit.[28]

The *Summa* devotes significant attention to the restoration of the divine image, setting the study of human nature and acts within a theological framework created by the New Law of the gospel. Following the narrative of salvation history, Aquinas describes human creatures' resemblance to God, the manner in which they imitate Christ as the way to salvation, and the degree to which they progress toward God in him. God's work in creation was to form human beings in his image by giving them the capacity to know and love him. The goal, moreover, is that humans will be led to fuller participation in the perfection of the divine image through contemplating the Father, Son, and Holy Spirit.[29]

The movement of human beings in responding to the divine initiative is primarily centered in the intellect and will, human faculties inclining toward truth and goodness and flowing from our spiritual nature to order our thoughts, affections, and actions toward God. The activity of the intellect, which speaks and forms ideas; and the movement of the will, which acts in love, are united in deliberative choice within the freedom of excellence that conforms us to Christ through the Spirit's grace.[30] Aquinas follows a long tradition that looks to the New Testament as its source (2 Peter 1:3–4).

> His divine power has given us everything needed for life and godliness, through the knowledge of him who called us to his own glory and goodness. Thus he has given us, through these things, his precious and very great promises, so that through them you may escape from the corruption that is in the world because of lust, and become participants in the divine nature.[31]

Only the mystery of grace is able to account for such radical change in human persons, just as grace is necessary to attain our final end in the knowledge and likeness of God's glory, "face to face." This participation begins with our baptism and justification, pertains in our present state, and will only be completed in the resurrection and life to come.[32] Commenting on Aquinas, Nicholas Healy describes grace in the following manner:

> Grace is the action of the Triune God that brings us into relation with God that so transforms and perfects the created relation that we live a new life in the Risen Christ. Grace originates with, and remains entirely dependent upon, the person and work of Christ, but it is by us and works in us through the power of the Holy Spirit, who draws us to the Father in the Son. . . . The grace of Jesus Christ is therefore necessary for us to achieve our proper end.[33]

Since every creature comes from God, each human person fulfills the requirement for being a true image of the Creator, which in turn, is inseparable from reflecting on Christ as fully embodying "the image of the invisible God, the first born of all creation."[34] For Aquinas, the image of God is the vital connection between his study of the work of God, human action, and morality as humanity's return to God. This in turn leads to the study of Christ who in his humanity is the way to God, while in his divine person is the Word of God, the perfect Image of the Father. Moreover, the image of God in humanity is dynamic, so that the processions of wisdom and love, as processions of intellect and will, are mirrored in the structures of human life by knowledge and affectivity. Through the gift of charity God becomes the source and object of understanding and affection, giving rise to the conception of words according to the intellect, and the procession of love according to the will.[35]

For this reason, the law of the gospel is neither an abstract message nor external law by virtue of its written form; the gospel is a law internal to the human person, originating in God's own self-knowledge and love and mediated by the presence and work of the Spirit. Drawing from the teaching of Scripture and the wisdom of Augustine, Aquinas defines the New Law as "the message of the Holy Spirit in the souls of the faithful," overflowing in the joy of speaking and acting well. Pinckaers comments:

> Having established the scriptural and patristic bases, Thomas now sets out to construct a nuanced answer: the New Law is an internal law by virtue of its main element, "The grace of the Holy Spirit." It is, nevertheless, external by virtue of certain secondary elements, which are like instruments of this grace. The principle element of the Law of the Gospel is the very same grace of the Holy Spirit, received through faith in Christ and love and along with these, by means of hope and the other virtues, that the Holy Spirit writes the New Law on the heart, in the lives of the faithful. All the energy of this law comes from the Holy Spirit. Thus the active principle of justification and of sanctification, of forgiveness and perfection is within us.[36]

Aquinas viewed the Sermon on the Mount as answering the question of human happiness. He considered the teaching of Christ, which regulates the interior acts of will, desire, and love according to the Spirit's grace, as the goal of knowing and preaching evangelical truth.[37] Aquinas also understood the sermon as inspiring Christians to imitate the holiness of the Teacher in becoming true lovers of Christ by following the way of beatitude in light of divine wisdom. As the wisdom of God taking root in human life, the sermon illumines the mind and heart through the Spirit's innermost workings, which radiate outward and order human words and actions through the law of the gospel.[38]

Aquinas's soteriological vision of the Old and New Law is "based upon Torah and Temple, interpreted in light of Christ." Salvation history consists in the perfection of the worship of God that culminates in eternal beatitude, the union of happiness and holiness which is "the point of Divine Law, Old and New."

> Thus at the heart of Thomas' theology of salvation lies the narrative of Scripture—the fulfillment of Israel's Torah and Temple through the New Covenant in Jesus Christ, which demonstrates the integral wisdom of sacred doctrine, investigating the nature of the Trinity, Jesus Christ, and human salvation. Thus Christ's perfect fulfillment of the Torah (wisdom) and Temple (holiness) are made one in the missions of the Son and Spirit, reconciling God and humanity, and allowing human beings to share, by the grace of the Spirit, in Christ's own self-giving of loving obedience and praise to the Father.[39]

According to Aquinas, such action is a source of joy, the affect of acting happily and wisely, with ease and pleasure; the joy with which we speak witnesses to God's saving activity and participates in God's goodness. J. P. Torrell comments:

> We are neither good nor virtuous if we do not find joy in acting well. To act or speak with joy is to do so with love so that we find delight in it. It is not sufficient to perform good acts and to say good things out of duty, obligation, or by following external rules; it must also be performed, done and said, with joy and delight according to the norm of the gospel itself.[40]

It would be difficult to overestimate the emphasis Aquinas places on spiritual joy as essential to the moral happiness made possible through the missions of Christ and the Spirit; since moral action is bound up with the highest forms of human activity and expressions of joy, pleasure, and delight.[41] For Thomas, happiness is constituted by the "joy of the truth," which surpasses sensate pleasure, utility, and sentimentality in generous openness and receptivity to the reality of God and others. The gift of friendship is received through the virtue of charity, God's love for us and the love by which we love God and neighbors, of which joy is both a present effect and a sign of future perfection.[42]

Wesley on Homiletic Happiness

John Wesley knew the tradition of virtue and happiness handed down in the work of Augustine and Aquinas.[43] As they did, he believed happiness is found in being restored to the image of God, which he understood as living in communion with God. For this reason, his teaching on the Christian life neither emphasizes mere obedience to external rules, principles, and commands, nor does it relegate faith to an internal private space. Interpreting Scripture according to the church's trinitarian doctrine, Wesley's vision of the Christian life was oriented by happy knowledge and holy living through the blessings pronounced by Jesus. He therefore read the Sermon on the Mount as an invitation to the way of holiness and happiness through faith in Christ and the Spirit's gifts and fruits. While the life of true religion requires external expressions such as doctrine, liturgy, and discipline, it will also entail internal gifts of faith, hope, love, joy, patience, peace, and goodness. Wesley describes this life in his exposition of the first Beatitude of Jesus:

> This is the kingdom of heaven or of God which is "within" us, even "righteousness, and peace, and joy in the Holy Ghost." And what is this righteousness but the life of God in the soul, the mind which was in Christ Jesus, the image of God stamped upon the heart, now renewed after the likeness of him that created it? What is it but the love of God because he first loved us, and the love of all mankind for his sake. And what is this but peace, the peace of God, but that calm serenity of soul, that sweet repose in the blood of Jesus, which leaves no doubt of our acceptance in him? Which excludes all fear but the loving, filial fear of offending our Father which is in heaven?[44]

Wesley's religion of the heart bears many similarities to the work of Augustine and Aquinas. They understood the end of God's commandment as love, not mere outward obedience, although this will be necessary, while not sufficient. Of greater importance is the empowerment of the tempers and passions that order our thoughts and actions to fulfill the law by knowing and doing the good and avoiding what is evil. Knowing the truth and doing the good is established by faith in the Teacher who is himself the Wisdom by which God restores us to the holy love in which we were created.

Stephen Long helpfully points out that Wesley preceded the discourses on the Sermon on the Mount with two sermons, "The Great Privilege of Those that Are Born of God" and "The Lord Our Righteousness." These sermons emphasize key themes in Wesley's moral theology, showing that the teaching of Jesus makes no sense without the virtues, gifts, and beatitudes, which themselves require their location in the trinitarian faith of the church. The key to reading the sermon is Jesus who speaks as truly God and truly human and yet one person. The sermon is therefore made intelligible by the Incarnation, the divine and human in Christ who grants knowledge of God's glory. "Only from this foundation in the Incarnation, can we dare to consider that the glory of God can be mediated through vision, smell, hearing, touch, and taste—not as they are in themselves, but as they become illumined and participatable as something other than themselves in Christ's Incarnation, Life, Crucifixion, Resurrection, and Ascension."[45]

This is the great privilege we share in Christ as our life is restored in the image of God by sanctifying grace and the infused virtues of faith, hope, and love, which is the way of moral happiness. This is:

> the life of God in the soul of a believer . . . wherein it properly consists, and what is immediately and necessarily implied therein. It immediately and necessarily implies the continual inspiration of God's Holy Spirit: God's breathing into the soul, and the soul's breathing back what it first receives from God; a continual action of God upon the soul, the re-action of the soul upon God; and unceasing presence of God, the loving pardoning God; manifested in the heart, and perceived by faith; and an unceasing return of love, praise, and prayer, offering up all our thoughts, all the words of our tongues, all the works of our hands, all our body, soul, and spirit, to be an holy sacrifice, acceptable unto God in Christ Jesus.[46]

Wesley's sermon "The Lord Our Righteousness" sets forth the trinitarian and christological basis of the Christian moral life. The fellowship of the

Father and the Son enables us to understand when we say the Lord our righteousness, in that Christ's human righteousness is imputed to us, and through this imputation we participate in the divine life, in a new way of life through faith in him; "love, love to the least of mankind, resignation to his Father, humility, gentleness, and every other holy and heavenly temper."[47] Long observes of these virtues:

> They are what Wesley means by "the religion of the heart." What must be emphasized is their Trinitarian form; love, reverence, and resignation to God describe the relationship between the First and Second Persons. Through Christ's human righteousness we are united into this same relationship. The Spirit draws us into it, for these virtues are not what is imputed, but this imputation becomes inherent in human nature. The possibility emerges from the Incarnation.[48]

This righteousness shapes Wesley's exposition of the Sermon on the Mount since the life and teaching of Jesus, his active righteousness, is to become our righteousness by his blessings and with the gifts of the Holy Spirit. As in the work of Augustine and Aquinas, Wesley's commentary on the way of holiness and happiness has a distinctive theological orientation; God incarnate is himself known as the way and goal, which has a soteriological and ethical orientation as well: "to assert and prove every branch of gospel obedience as indispensably necessary to eternal salvation."[49]

The beginning of the first discourse sets the stage for what follows. Wesley calls attention to who it is that is speaking so that we may "take heed how we hear." He continues, "It is the Lord of heaven and earth, the Creator of all, who as such, has a right to dispose of all his creatures; the lord our Govenor, whose kingdom is everlasting, and ruleth over all." The Teacher is the "Eternal Wisdom of the Father." He is no mere human teacher, but the One "who knows whereof we are made, who understands our innermost being, how we stand related to God, one another, and all creatures, and indeed knows how to adapt every law to fit the circumstances in which we find ourselves."[50] Thus to know and love him is to see the order and wisdom of things.

Or to put his differently, Jesus is God's practical wisdom through whom God providentially orders and accomplishes all things according to his good purpose. Wesley affirms he is the "God of Love," who "emptied himself of his glory, coming forth from the Father to teach God's will to the children of men and to return to the Father." And this was done to "open the eyes of the blind and to give light to those who sit in darkness." Following in the tradition of Augustine and Aquinas, Wesley presents the authority and ethos of Jesus as the Teacher of righteousness, asserting he is both the message and the messenger who mediates God's truth and fulfills God's law through the perfection of his love. "He is the incarnate Son who came from heaven to show us the way to heaven, the true way to life everlasting, the royal way that leads to the kingdom." Wesley reads the Sermon on the Mount in light of the Incarnation, as an address to Israel, to the church, to the nations, and "all the generations to come, even to the end of the world."[51] As the Wisdom of creation and redemption, Christ illumines the world with the glory of God, the Creator and Redeemer.

In addition to ethos (the character of the speaker) and the logos (the message of the speaker), Wesley also comments on pathos (the manner of the speaker): "How our Lord teaches here." Wesley compares him to the prophets and apostles who in degree of heavenly wisdom are only the Lord's servants. In all of Scripture there is nothing else that compares with "the whole plan of his religion," the "full prospect of Christianity," which describes "at large the nature of that holiness without which no one shall see the Lord." In Jesus, the preacher, what is preached, and the manner of preaching are one.[52]

According to Wesley, nothing else in Scripture can compare with this teaching other than the sketch of holiness given to Moses in the commandments. However, there remains a wide difference between these two preachers; the glory of Christ includes but also exceeds the law of Moses as Jesus speaks in a manner that is more than human: "It speaks the Creator of all—a God, a God appears!, Yea, . . . the being of beings, Jehovah, the self-existent, the supreme, the God who is over all, blessed for ever!" This is the "still, small voice of God" speaking to all who long for life, for goodness, for wisdom, for happiness, for peace, and to experience the joy of heaven below and heaven above. This is the way of happiness: "Blessed (or happy) are the poor in spirit. Happy are the mourners, the meek; those that hunger after righteousness: the merciful, the pure in heart: happy in the end and in the Way; happy in this life and in life everlasting!"[53]

The Beatitudes speak to the deepest desires and aspirations of the human heart because the Teacher himself is the Eternal Law, the Second Person of the Trinity, truly God and truly human in one Person who shares his righteousness and bestows his blessedness to make us holy and happy. Wesley sees the first six beatitudes as the religion of the heart, or what Christians are to be. This is consistent with the teaching of Augustine and Aquinas, taking into account the Beatitudes, the gifts of the Spirit, the virtues of faith, hope, and love, and the Spirit's fruit. This is inward holiness. It is to be expressed in all outward actions and conversation, "Blessed are the peacemakers, for they shall be called children of God."[54] Being, as inward holiness, precedes doing; just as external religion requires inward religion.[55]

In Wesley's reading, the life of blessedness that is spoken and modeled by Christ is both deeply personal and inescapably social, uniting piety and public witness. Moreover, this is the work of faith and the labor of love that seeks to do all manner of good by extending every blessing to body and soul in all manner of material and spiritual conditions. In addition, this is the fruit of God's undeserved love and favor that energize every good work that God has prepared for those that love him. God is pleased to share his goodness and happiness through the works and words of those who serve as instruments in his hand. Filled with love of God and all humankind, peacemakers happily embody a calm, patient, assuring, reconciling presence in the world, fulfilling the law through the holy love wherein we were created and which is our final end in Christ.[56]

The last blessing points to what those who seek peace and to do all manner of good in the world should expect, "Blessed are they which are persecuted for righteousness sake; for theirs is the kingdom of heaven." The spirit of the world is opposed to the Spirit of God, but is overcome by the religion of the heart spreading virtue and happiness throughout the world: love, meekness, gentleness, goodness, and forgiveness, patience, longsuffering, mercy and kindness. Wesley concludes, "Be, 'Christians' perfect (in kind though not degree) even as your Father in heaven is perfect."[57]

Wesley summarizes the teaching of the Beatitudes as the "genuine religion of Jesus Christ" and "Christianity in its native form as delivered by its Author." Those whose eyes are opened by the divine wisdom taught by Christ are enabled to see God in human form, as imitable by human creatures. Expressing delight in the beauty, proportion, and fittingness between the parts and the whole of Christ's wisdom, Wesley exclaims, "How desirable is the happiness here described! How venerable, how lovely the holiness!" As the spirit of true religion and the foundation of Christianity, Christ's blessings are to be received and transcribed in the heart till "we are holy as he which hath called us is holy."[58]

Situated at the theological center of *Sermons on Several Occasions*, Wesley's exposition of the Beatitudes epitomizes the purpose of the whole: to describe the true, scriptural "religion of the heart" in the expression of homiletic theology: the joy of knowing the truth in living faith and fulfilling the law by loving God and neighbor. Such virtuous and happy preaching springs from faith in the One who "came down from heaven" to teach the way of God who "prepar[es] us for the knowledge of all truth, by filling our hearts with all his love, and with all joy and peace in believing."[59] The truth of God matters in preaching.

CHAPTER 7

PREACHING THEOLOGIANS

This book has called attention to Wesley as a "preaching theologian" and exemplar of the practice of preaching in which the Holy Spirit awakens us to the joy of hearing God's Word. Such enjoyment constitutes a useless, noninstrumental, participative activity, with no purpose other than delighting in the extravagant, outpouring of love through which the Father communicates his being and life to the Son, who through the work of the Spirit restores human creatures to the divine image.

Because Wesley understood the end of human life as conformance to the image of Christ through the gifts of justifying and sanctifying grace, human actions—including the act of preaching—are true and good when directed to God who is known and loved for his own sake, rather than a means to achieving something else. At the heart of Wesley's vision is a conviction that our truest end is to know and love God, so that the witness of preaching will spring from and lead back to doxology—the praise of God's glory—rather than a preacher's relevance, effectiveness, or skills. In other words, the activity of preaching and the goal of preaching are one; rendering faithful, public witness to the gospel of Jesus Christ through the presence and work of the Spirit in the worshiping life of the church.

In contrast to modern "liberal" and "conservative" expressions of Christianity, for Wesley the ministry of the church was not instrumental for achieving ends other than love for God and neighbor. My hope is that attending to Wesley as a "preaching theologian" has shown the need for preachers to be schooled in the "grammar" of faith so that our preaching will be congruent with the truth of the church's trinitarian confession. In other words, rather than simply attempting to repeat what Wesley said, did, and accomplished, our task is to discern the wisdom of Wesley's faith and practice in order to discern and judge best how to think and speak in ways that are both faithful to God and fitting for the church's mission within the conditions and circumstances of our time.

119

Andrew Moore has persuasively argued that the language and "grammar" of faith is learned through the Triune God's involvement in human life. It is not primarily from theology that we learn the correct use of Christian discourse, but rather from *God's* saving activity among his people through the Spirit of Jesus. *God* is the grammar of faith, since it is the Triune God in the person of Christ and through the power of the Spirit, who teaches what cannot be learned from practices or rules.

Christian doctrine, which is integrally related to the interpretation of Scripture, is inseparable from that which it informs and guides—the church's embodiment, enactment, and performance of the gospel in coming to know, love, and obey God; a kind of "habituated" knowledge that enables us to speak the truth in love. Thus without God's incarnate activity there would be no Christian discourse, since it is Christ to whom all Christian practice intends: "The material context of the grammar of faith is the presence of God in Christ . . . the church bears faithful witness to God's language spoken in Christ by the Spirit's declaring and enacting God's conforming of the world to his word according to the wisdom of Christ."[1]

For Wesley, speaking of God is the effect of a prior grace; the divine being and goodness communicated through the incarnate Word and the witness of the Spirit who engender faith that comes by hearing.[2] Guided by the law of the gospel through the witness of the Spirit, preaching seeks to imitate the manner of God's speaking in Jesus Christ as mediated by the whole of Scripture. For Wesley, then, sermons were the primary place for doing theology to communicate the knowledge and love of God. He affirmed this commitment while addressing the church's "effectiveness" in bearing witness to God's self-communication in Christ.

> Why has Christianity done so little good in the world? Is it not the balm which the Great Physician has given to men, to restore their spiritual health? . . . I am bold to affirm, that those who bear the name of Christ are in general totally ignorant, both to the theory and practice of Christianity; so that they are "perishing by thousands for lack of knowledge experience . . . of justification by faith, the new birth, inward and outward holiness."[3]

As a "preaching theologian," Wesley helps us to see more clearly the practical wisdom of Christian doctrine—the truth confessed by the church according to the scriptural witness to God's goodness in the whole narrative of creation, fall, incarnation, and new creation—through which the witness of the Holy Spirit transforms us to participate in the divine nature. In other words, Wesley unites theory and practice in habits of thought, life, and speech that are learned through loving devotion to the Father in the Spirit who draws us to the truth of Christ.

Wesley was the reluctant founder of an evangelical order of preachers who came to prominence during the eighteenth century in response to an urgent need for doctrinally informed and ecclesially grounded evangelism, catechesis, and discipleship (thus sharing many similarities with our time).[4] The aim of "Methodist" preaching was to evangelize those not yet converted, and to exhort, onto holiness of life, the justified who were supposed to be "going on to perfection." Fundamental for Wesley was the conviction that living faith and genuine holiness are the fruit of God's self-giving through the Word and Spirit indwelling the life of the church. Recognizing that a world without saints will not know how to praise, know, and obey the Triune God who is its source and end, Wesley furthered this mission by providing written sermons as examples of homiletic wisdom that united conversion and discipleship, faith and good works, love and the law, grace and the virtues.

This amounted to a great deal, as Wesley expected Methodist preachers to spend significant time in prayer and study for "transcribing" the knowledge of Christ into habits of virtuous life and speech. The centerpiece of Wesley's homiletic pedagogy was his collections of sermons for guiding preachers to assist the Spirit's work of calling and forming disciples of Jesus Christ within a common life of doctrine, devotion, and discipleship. If, for Wesley, oral sermons were to serve proclamation, invitation, and conversion to Christ, written sermons were for nurture and education; training in knowing how to "preach Christ" in specific times and places according to the practical wisdom that we are to love God and our neighbors. Randy Maddox comments on Wesley's concern that preachers would possess the necessary practical knowledge for preaching Christ "in all his offices" in order to inculcate a *pattern* or *grammar* of faith that works through the joyful obedience and love.

The fact that Wesley's concern surfaced in relation to preaching suggests a preferable way of putting this point: the doctrine of the Three Offices [Prophet, Priest, and King] served for Wesley as a "grammar" for norming practical—theological activities aimed at forming the beliefs, affection and practices of his people. . . . He wanted to insure that God's grace known in Christ as Priest was never separated from the response of discipleship that Christ modeled as Prophet and calls for from his followers as King.[5]

Theology serves the preaching of the gospel, just as preaching is the expression of theology which "offers Christ" through whom the Spirit imparts the gifts of knowledge and love which are able to make us holy and happy in God.[6] Wesley writes:

We may learn, hence, . . . that this happy knowledge of the true God is only another name for religion; I mean Christian religion, which indeed is the only one that deserves the name. Religion, as to the nature or essence of it, does not lie in this or that set of notions, vulgarily called "faith"; nor in a round of duties, however carefully "reformed" from error or superstition. It does not consist in any number of outward actions. No; it properly and directly consists in the knowledge and love of God, as manifested in the Son of his love, through the eternal Spirit. And this naturally leads to every heavenly temper, and to every good word and work.[7]

William Abraham notes of Wesley, "In an inimitable and wonderful way he [Wesley] helped people find God in conversion, became a model for them of the spiritual life, and provided a network of resources to nourish genuine holiness."[8] Preaching was doxological speech; the declaration of thankful praise evoked by the Father's love through the Son in the power of the Spirit who raises up the church to bear visible witness to the divine mission in the world, the *missio Dei*. Lutheran theologian Martin Schmidt comments, "He [Wesley] was the first in the whole course of church history who realized that the task of Christendom in the modern world is to be defined as mission."[9]

Wesley's sermons invite us into a theological conversation initiated by the Father's self-communication in the Son through whom the Spirit calls, pardons, regenerates and sanctifies the church across time. Although Wesley's work has been studied by historians, theologians, evangelists, and scholars of liturgics, ethics and spirituality, his work as a homiletic theologian and exemplar of the "preaching life" deserves renewed attention from students, preachers, and homileticians. As the leader of a significant preaching movement, Wesley exemplified the character of faith, love, goodness, and happiness that constituted the message and mission of Methodism from its beginnings. We may yet learn of such things from Wesley by allowing him to be our teacher in "a school of desire and wisdom which is concerned with both God and the world and within which people can be formed in faith, hope and love . . . to live in the Spirit."[10] Albert Outler writes of Wesley's vision of message and mission:

> Speak as ardently as you will of the primacy of mission over doctrine (in my view, a wholly gratuitous disjunction), and it is still true that the Christian message is the Christian mission and that the measure of mission is not mission itself but rather the hearing of faith (cf. Rom. 10:17). If it is true . . . that Methodists have, or had, a distinctive understanding of what goes into the "hearing of faith," then it would follow that our particular understanding of that message affects our understanding of the Christian message.[11]

To Live by Preaching

For Wesley, the witness of preaching is inseparable from an ecclesial identity and way of life that is constituted by the grace of Jesus Christ, the love of God, and the communion of the Holy Spirit. This way of life attains its maturity through the cultivation of sound knowledge and vital piety; the mind, where wisdom dwells; the will, which loves; the imagination and sensibilities, which perceive; the affections and passions, which order our lives to share in God's good work through joyful action and speech. In other words, hearing and speaking God's Word is primarily a matter of having our attention and theological judgment formed in congruence with the character of holiness.

In speaking of holiness we are dealing with a pattern of knowing and loving embodied by Christ and communicated by the Spirit through preaching and the other means of grace.[12] According to Wesley, this entails participation in Christ's human righteousness that restores our hearts and satisfies our desire for communion with God.

The human righteousness of Christ belongs to him in his human nature, as he is "the mediator between God and man, the man Christ Jesus." This is either internal or external. His internal righteousness is the image of God stamped on every power and faculty of the soul. It is a copy of his divine righteousness, as far as it can be imparted to a human spirit. It is a transcript of the divine purity, the divine justice, mercy and truth. It includes love, reverence, resignation to his Father; humility, meekness, gentleness; love to lost mankind, and every other kind of holy and heavenly temper: and all these in the highest degree, without any defect, or mixture of unholiness.[13]

Writing of all who confess the name of Christ and stand under the Christian law—the law of the gospel—Wesley asserts, "unless these be so changed . . . unless they have new senses, ideas, passions, tempers, they are no Christians! However just, true, or merciful they may be, they are atheists still."[14] In other words, morality and all the justice, mercy, and truth that exist are of no profit in themselves, since without the transformation of our habits, passions, and tempers by the work of Christ and the Holy Spirit, we are still but "practical atheists."

Wesley's concern addresses what is arguably the most neglected aspect of contemporary homiletics: the transformation of a preacher's life and speech by the living Word we confess and proclaim. Preaching is an evangelical message and way of life that is shaped by the Word of God in Christ whose presence is mediated by Scripture within the life of the church. Wesley's practical wisdom directs our attention to the living God who, through the work of grace, engenders the virtues of faith, hope, and love, the Spirit's gifts and fruit, and the way of discipleship pronounced by Jesus that leads to happiness and the perfection of love. For this reason, learning to preach will entail becoming a certain kind of person who loves the truth and knows how to speak the truth in particular times and places. In other words, the practice of preaching is inseparable from the calling that all Christians share: "work out your salvation with fear and trembling."

Or to put this differently, becoming a preacher will entail sharing in "the mind of Christ" through the work of the Holy Spirit who purifies the eyes of our hearts to discern and describe the truth of things: "But the moment the Spirit of the Almighty strikes the heart of that was till then without God in the world, it breaks the hardness of his heart, and creates all things new. The sun of righteousness appears, and shines upon his soul. . . . He is in a new world. All things round him are become new."[15] Wesley continues:

> By the same gracious stroke, he that before had ears but heard not is now made capable of hearing. He hears the voice that raiseth the dead, the voice of him that is the resurrection and the life. He is no longer deaf to his invitations and commands, to his promises or threatenings, but gladly hears every word that proceeds out of his mouth.[16]

My hope is that in our need for liberation from cultural captivity we may learn from Wesley as a preaching theologian and exemplar of the preaching life. In so doing, we may be surprised to discover Wesley's "relevance" for our time, when the efficacy of preaching has become increasingly dependent upon the production of contemporary relevance, or *sola cultura* (culture alone), through strategies that consist of indentifying needs and choosing goals on terms established by the religious economy in American culture.

By *sola cultura*, I am referring to dependence upon methods and strategies that seek their justification in the privileges or advantages derived from cultural accommodation and consumer approval—rather than the knowledge of faith which is communicated by the grace of the risen Christ through the Spirit indwelling the church. Wesley, on the other hand, encourages us toward cultivating a way of thinking, speaking, and living that springs from faith, is active in love, and seeks to share in the goodness and happiness of God: "As faith is in order to love, so love is in order to goodness—and so also goodness is in order to blessedness."[17] Emphasizing "the holiness without which no man shall see the Lord" in a sermon from his latter years, Wesley writes:

> The righteousness of Christ is, doubtless, necessary for any soul that enters into glory. But so is personal holiness, too, for every child of man. But it is highly needful to observe that they are necessary in different respects. The former is necessary to entitle us to heaven; the latter, to qualify us for it. Without the righteousness of Christ we could have no claim to glory; without holiness we could have no fitness for it. By the former we are members of Christ, children of God, and heirs of the kingdom of heaven. By the latter we are "made meet to be partakers of the inheritance of the saints in light."[18]

The time is right for returning to Wesley's practical wisdom in the Scripture way of salvation. As Abraham argues, if it is true that we are nearing "the end of Wesleyan theology" after a generation-long search for the "historical Wesley," [then]:

> as a specific, determinate experiment in the history of Western theology, Methodism is now over. This does not mean the institutions and ecclesial bodies invented by Wesley and his followers have ceased to exist; these will continue to wind their way through the course of history best they can. My point is a simple one. The historical investigation of the last thirty years constitutes a very long obituary notice . . . [in that] the missiological agenda of Wesley, together with the practices that were constitutive of it, has been abandoned . . . the circle of criticism for within have eaten away the background theological assumptions on which Wesley critically depended, so that there is now in place a pluralism of background assumptions that do the theologically heavy lifting. The material theologies that result, and that are now clearly visible, are only secondarily Wesleyan. Their deep inspiration and their core commitments are derived from non-Wesleyan sources.[19]

Stephen Long describes the modern intellectual habits that have led to the end of Wesleyan theology and "ethics" as a state of affairs that renders God irrelevant by policing theology out of social and political concerns. The tradition of "social ethics" which emerged in the early twentieth century did so within arrangements that valued theology primarily for its usefulness to the formative powers of culture, the nation, and market according to technical wisdom that works by criteria of the social sciences. Long concludes that our contemporary quests to secure Wesley's "relevance" for "today" have only perpetuated the asocial, apolitical nature of theology and the modern "irrelevance" in which his doctrinal and moral convictions remain trapped.[20]

In the sermon "On the Unity of Divine Being" Wesley addresses the displacement of the Three-One God by forms of "enlightened" religion; morality derived from reason and experience which is represented by self-sufficient humanisms separated from knowing, loving, and enjoying God.

> Thus almost all men of letters, both in England, France and Germany, yea, and all the civilized countries of Europe, extol "humanity" to the skies, as the very

essence of religion. That this great triumvirate, Rousseau, Voltaire, and David Hume, have contributed all their labours, sparing no pains to establish a religion which should stand on its own foundation, independent of any revelation whatever, yea, not supposing even the being of a God. So leaving him, if he has any being, to himself, they have found out both a religion and a happiness which have no relation at all to God, nor any dependence upon him. It is no wonder that this religion should grow fashionable, and spread far and wide in the world. But call it "humanity," "virtue," "morality," or what you please, it is neither, better or worse than atheism. Men hereby willfully and designedly put asunder what God has joined, the duties of the first and second table. It is separating the love of our neighbor from the love of God. It is a plausible way of thrusting God out of the world he has made.[21]

Following the language and grammar of faith, Wesley identifies the activity of Christ and the Spirit who transform our being and life in the knowledge and love of God. This is a kind of "habituated knowledge" that precludes its function as a technical device that "works" by means of autonomous understanding and desire. Wesley saw the existence of Christian people, including preachers, as dependent upon the

life of God in the soul of a believer [which] is . . . a continual action of God upon the soul, the reaction of the soul upon God; an unceasing presence of God, the loving, pardoning God, manifested in the heart, and perceived by faith; and an unceasing return of love, praise, and prayer, offering up all the thoughts of our hearts, all the words of our tongues, all the works of our hands, all our body, soul, and spirit, to be an holy sacrifice, acceptable unto God in Christ Jesus.[22]

Such spiritual and moral sensibilities are the fruit of personal knowledge in Christian doctrine and a way of life that joins passionate commitment to Christ with public witness to the reign of God through the social embodiment of holiness. Through constancy in the gifts of faith, hope, and love, we are transformed to know the Father who has made us and redeemed us to be his beloved children through the grace of Christ and the Spirit of adoption. In other words, our participation in the mind of Christ is both a relational and intellectual activity that enables discernment of, and participation in, the truth of creation and redemption.

This way of being entails a participation in the Son through the work of the Spirit who illumines our minds with wisdom of Scripture according to the analogy of faith. It is significant that Wesley does separate knowledge and spirituality, faith and the moral life, Scripture and interpretation, or grace and virtue. Preaching is an integrative activity that springs from the obedience of love through the life of religion as communicated by the "oracles of God." Wesley writes of its nature:

> According to these [Scripture] it lies in one single point: it is neither more nor less than love—it is love which "is the fulfilling of the law," "the end of the commandment." Religion is the love of God and our neighbour—that is, every man under heaven. This love, ruling the whole life, animating our tempers and passions, directing all our thoughts, words, and actions, is "pure religion and undefiled."[23]

The message of Wesley's sermons was the primary medium for communicating what Methodists believed, were about, and hoped to become by the presence and work of Jesus Christ and of the Holy Spirit in the life of the church. Within the economy of salvation, the sanctifying work of the Spirit involves us in the appointed means that convey the power of grace and serve as disciplines for living in love with God and neighbor; a transformation made intelligible by the church's trinitarian confession. In other words, the announcement of the Father's loving self-giving, mediated by the Son through the outpouring of the Spirit, springs from and leads to a common life of doctrine, devotion, and discipline that is our means of returning to God the life we receive from God as a sacrifice of thanks and praise.

Such tempers, affections, and passions constitute the content and scope of Wesley's sermons—"the essentials of true religion,"[24]—which seek to communicate the faith that works through love.[25] As Wesley writes in the 1746 preface to *Sermons on Several Occasions*, "May [God] prepare us for the knowledge of all truth, by filling our hearts with all his love, and with all joy and peace in believing." God's work does not negate the importance of the preacher's work in preaching. While God and human creatures are distinct, they are not in competition. The Holy Spirit works in, with, and through a preacher's life and words, imparting the gifts of faith and love that come by hearing and receiving the Word with joy. As Mark McIntosh notes, "This freely self-giving love of Christ becomes, by the power of the Holy Spirit, the very structure of a new kind of talking and thinking and being with one another."[26]

Thus the more we attend to God through faith in Christ the more we will know him, and the more we know him the more we will be drawn to him in love, and the more we are drawn to him in love the more our thoughts, acts, and words will be conformed to the truth of the incarnate Word who is the source and end of our life.[27] As Geoffrey Wainwright comments, "The dynamic link between love of God and neighbor is established by Wesley," as it was summed up by St. Augustine: *initari quem colis*, "to imitate Him whom you worship."[28]

John Wesley was not a good "modern" theologian, exegete, or preacher. Rather his work unites these "modern" disciplines in devotion to God that includes intellectual and moral virtues. For this reason, his work may yet challenge us to see that modernity's advances in empirical knowledge, its increasing dependence upon the power of effectiveness, and its orientation by the logic of technological thinking, ingenuity, and skill, have not nurtured the virtues of faith, hope, and love that engender the "mind of Christ"—the pattern of knowing and loving that all creatures are called to share.[29]

As a homiletic theologian, Wesley's life and preaching were oriented by the gifts of faith and love by which the Spirit purifies the eyes of our heart and understanding to speak truthfully of God, ourselves, others, and the world. In a sermon during the latter years of his ministry, Wesley inquires, "What is Methodism? What does this new word mean? Is it not a new religion? . . . Methodism, so called, is the old religion, the religion of the Bible, the religion of the primitive church, the religion of the Church of England." He continues:

And this is the religion of the Church of England, as appears from all her authentic records, from the uniform tenor of her liturgy, and from numberless passages in her Homilies. . . . The scriptural primitive religion of love, . . . is beautifully summed up in that one comprehensive petition, "Cleanse the thoughts of our hearts by the inspiration of thy Holy Spirit, that we may perfectly love thee, and worthily magnify thy holy name."[30]

Introduction: A Homiletic Theologian

1. William Abraham, "The End of Wesleyan Theology," *Wesleyan Theological Journal*, 40:1 (Spring 2005): 19.

2. Albert Outler, *The Wesleyan Theological Heritage: Essays of Albert C. Outler*, ed. Thomas C. Oden and Leicester R. Longden (Grand Rapids, MI: Zondervan, 1991), 53–54.

3. Richard Lischer, *Preacher King: Martin Luther King Jr. and the Word that Moved America* (Oxford: Oxford University Press, 1995), offers a model for this kind of study. I have attempted to do so in Michael Pasquarello III, "Hugh Latimer, God's Ploughman: A Preaching Life (1490–1555)" (PhD diss., University of North Carolina, 2002; Carlisle: Paternoster, forthcoming).

4. In my reading for this project I have been instructed by D. Stephen Long, *John Wesley's Moral Theology: The Quest for God and Goodness* (Nashville: Abingdon, 2005); Randy L. Maddox, *Responsible Grace: John Wesley's Practical Theology* (Nashville: Abingdon, 1994); Thomas A. Langford, *Practical Divinity: Theology in the Wesleyan Tradition* (Nashville: Abingdon, 1983), vol. 1; Richard P. Heitzenrater, *Wesley and the People Called Methodists* (Nashville: Abingdon, 1995); Scott J. Jones, *John Wesley's Conception and Use of Scripture* (Nashville: Abingdon, 1995); Ted A. Campbell, *John Wesley and Christian Antiquity: Religious Vision and Cultural Change* (Nashville: Abingdon, 1991); Mark L. Weeter, *John Wesley's View and Use of Scripture* (Eugene, OR: Wipf and Stock, 2007); *The Place of Wesley in the Christian Tradition: Essays Delivered at Drew University in Celebration of the Commencement of the Publication of the Oxford Edition of the Works of John Wesley*, ed. Kenneth E. Rowe (Metuchen, NJ: Scarecrow, 1976); William J. Abraham, *Wesley for Armchair Theologians* (Louisville: Westminster/John Knox, 2005); Jason E. Vickers, *Wesley: A Guide for the Perplexed* (London and New York: T&T Clark, 2009); *Reading the Bible in Wesleyan Ways: Some Constructive Proposals*, ed. Barry L. Callen and Richard P. Thompson (Kansas City, MO: Beacon Hill, 2004); Geoffrey Wainwright, *Methodists in Dialog* (Nashville: Abingdon, 1995); Robert E. Cushman, *John Wesley's Experimental Divinity: Studies in Methodist Doctrinal Standards* (Nashville: Abingdon, 1989); Albert Outler, *The Wesleyan Theological Heritage: Essays of*

Albert C. Outler, ed. Thomas C. Oden and Leicester R. Longden (Grand Rapids, MI: Zondervan, 1991); Kenneth J. Collins, *The Theology of John Wesley: Holy Love and the Shape of Grace* (Nashville: Abingdon, 2007).

5. I have attempted to identify the "grammar" of preaching in Michael Pasquarello III, *We Speak Because We Have First Been Spoken: A Grammar of the Preaching Life* (Grand Rapids, MI: Eerdmans, 2009). My hope is that readers will look to Wesley as a mentor in the ministry of the gospel for the purpose of making Christians and nurturing them into the fullness of the Christian life.

6. This is similar to the description given in Nicholas M. Healy, *Thomas Aquinas: Theologian of the Christian Life* (Aldershot, UK, and Burlington, VT: Ashgate, 2003), 33. I have learned much from Healy's account of Thomas as a theologian of the Christian life.

7. See the collection of essays situating Methodism within a larger ecumenical context by Geoffrey Wainwright, *Methodists in Dialog* (Nashville: Abingdon, 1995).

8. *The Bicentennial Edition of the Works of John Wesley*, ed. Albert C. Outler (Nashville: Abingdon, 1984–), 2:68. Hereafter referred to as *Works*.

9. I find it interesting that many who call themselves "Wesleyan" understand this to mean that the primary measure of ministry is contemporary "relevance." They do not seem to realize that this apologetic strategy was one that Wesley strongly opposed since it reduced religion to morality. In the name of making God "relevant" on terms defined by the "contemporary" or "with the times," they continue to work within Enlightenment categories that have made God and theology useless or irrelevant, policed out of public life into a private, "spiritual" sphere.

10. Daniel L. Burnett, *In the Shadow of Aldersgate: An Introduction to the Heritage and Faith of the Wesleyan Tradition* (Eugene, OR: Cascade Books, 2006), 113.

11. *Works*, 2:499.

12. See the extended argument in Charles Taylor, *A Secular Age* (Cambridge and London: The Belknap Press of Harvard University Press, 2007), 17.

13. Long, *John Wesley's Moral Theology*, 5.

14. *Works*, 1:105–6.

15. Eugene H. Peterson, *Under the Unpredictable Plant: An Exploration in Vocational Holiness* (Grand Rapids, MI: Eerdmans; Leicester: Gracewing, 1992).

16. Eugene H. Peterson, *Eat This Book: A Conversation in the Art of Spiritual Reading* (Grand Rapids, MI: Eerdmans, 2006), 107.

17. Peterson, *Under the Unpredictable Plant*, 21.

18. *Works*, 3:99.

19. Robert Louis Wilken, *The Spirit of Early Christian Thought: Seeking the Face of God* (New Haven, CT, and London: Yale University Press, 2003), 172.

20. Ibid., 173, 180.

21. William J. Abraham, "The End of Wesleyan Theology," *Wesleyan Theological Journal* 40:1 (Spring 2005): 21.

22. *Works*, 3:96.

23. Richard Lischer, introduction to *The Company of Preachers: Wisdom on Preaching, Augustine to the Present*, ed. Richard Lischer (Grand Rapids, MI: Eerdmans, 2002), xiv.

24. Stanley Hauerwas, "Carving Stone and Learning to Speak Christian" in *The State of the University: Academic Knowledges and the Knowledge of God* (Malden, MA and Oxford: Blackwell, 2007), 121.

25. Long, *John Wesley's Moral Theology*, 14–16.

26. Abraham, "The End of Wesleyan Theology," 17–18.

27. Albert C. Outler, *Evangelism and Theology in the Wesleyan Spirit* (Nashville: Discipleship Resources, 1996), 34.

28. Cited in W. L. Doughty, *John Wesley: Preacher* (London: Epworth, 1955), 194.

29. Charles M. Wood, *An Invitation to Theological Study* (Valley Forge, PA: Trinity, 1994), 105, 107.

30. Bishop Kenneth Carder writes, "The sociology of church growth has replaced the theology of personal and social transformation. It is indeed a sad commentary that United Methodist preachers are more familiar with pop sociology than with the theology of John Wesley. This preoccupation with institutional power and statistics contributes to preaching that is heavy on institutional promotion and narcissistic self-help and light on individual and communal salvation." Cf. "Proclaiming the Gospel of Grace" in *Theology and Evangelism in the Wesleyan Heritage*, ed. James C. Logan (Nashville: Abingdon, 1994).

31. Julian N. Hartt, *Toward a Theology of Evangelism* (Eugene, OR: Wipf and Stock, repr. 2006), 117.

32. Cited in Outler, introduction to *Works*, 1:13.

33. *Works*, 4:70.

34. Albert Outler, *The Wesleyan Theological Heritage: Essays of Albert C. Outler* (Grand Rapids, MI: Zondervan, 1991), 53.

35. William J. Abraham, "The Revitalization of United Methodist Doctrine and the Renewal of Evangelism" in *Theology and Evangelism in the Wesleyan Heritage*, ed. James C. Logan (Nashville: Abingdon, 1994), 49.

36. Cited in Abraham, "The End of Wesleyan Theology."

37. Nicholas Lash, *Voices of Authority* (Eugene, OR: Wipf and Stock, 2005), 11–12.

38. "An Address to the Clergy," *The Works of John Wesley*, 3rd. ed., repr. (Grand Rapids, MI: Baker, 1978), 488–89.

39. On the significance of describing the history of Christian practice as a guide for the present, see George A. Lindbeck, "Atonement and the Hermeneutics of Intratextual Social Embodiment" in *Evangelicals and Postliberals in Conversation*, ed. Timothy R. Phillips and Dennis L. Okholm (Downers Grove, IL: InterVarsity, 1996). See the argument for the recovery of tradition in Jaroslav Pelikan, *The Vindication of Tradition* (New Haven, CT: Yale University Press, 1984); Stephen R. Holmes, *Listening to the Past: The Place of Tradition in Theology* (Grand Rapids, MI: Baker Academic, 2002).

40. Long, *John Wesley's Moral Theology*, 173.

41. Ibid., xvii.

42. Jaroslav Pelikan, *Divine Rhetoric: The Sermon on the Mount as Message and Model in Augustine, Chrysostom, and Luther* (Crestwood, NY: St. Vladimir's Seminary Press, 2001), 56–57.

43. W. L. Doughty, *John Wesley: Preacher* (London: Epworth, 1955); Albert Outler, introduction to *Works*, 1:1–100, provides a more recent and comprehensive framework for approaching Wesley's sermons.

1. The Practice of Wisdom

1. "An Address to the Clergy," *The Works of John Wesley*, 3rd ed. (Grand Rapids, MI: Baker, 1978), 488.

2. Daniel A. Keating, "Justification, Sanctification, and Divinization in Thomas Aquinas," in *Aquinas on Doctrine*, ed. Thomas G. Weinandy, OFM, Daniel A. Keating, and John Y. Yocum (London and New York: T&T Clark, 2004), 152–55; Matthew L. Lamb, "The Eschatology of St. Thomas," in *Aquinas on Doctrine*, 226.

3. Servais Pinckaers, "Reappropriating Aquinas's Account of the Passions," in *The Pinckaers Reader: Renewing Thomistic Moral Theology*, ed, John Berkman and Craig Steven Titus, trans. Mary Thomas Noble (Washington, DC: Catholic University of America Press, 2005), 285–86; Lamb, "The Eschatology of St. Thomas," 225.

4. Edward Farley, *Theologia: The Fragmentation and Unity of Theological Education* (Philadelphia: Fortress, 1983), 33–39; see also the survey and definition of theology in Aidan Nichols, O.P., *The Shape of Catholic Theology: An Introduction to Its Sources, Principles, and History* (Collegeville, MN: Liturgical, 1991).

5. Bryan Stone, *Evangelism after Christendom: The Theology and Practice of Christian Witness* (Grand Rapids, MI: Brazos, 2007), 15–16.

6. Geoffrey Wainwright, *Methodists in Dialog* (Nashville: Abingdon, 1995), 283–84.

7. On Wesleyan spirituality see the essay by Geoffrey Wainwright, "Trinitarian Theology and Wesleyan Holiness," in *Orthodox and Wesleyan Spirituality*, ed. S. T. Kimbrough (Crestwood, NY: St. Vladimir's Seminary Press, 2002), 59–80.

8. David S. Cunningham, *Faithful Persuasion: In Aid of a Rhetoric of Christian Theology* (Notre Dame, IN: University of Notre Dame Press, 1991), 107.

9. D. Stephen Long, *John Wesley's Moral Theology: The Quest for God and Goodness* (Nashville: Abingdon, 2005), 174.

10. *Works*, 4:70–71.

11. Dunne, *Back to the Rough Ground: Practical Judgment and the Lure of Technique* (Notre Dame, IN: University of Notre Dame Press, 1993), 378.

12. Michael Dauphinias and Matthew Levering, *Knowing the Love of Christ: An Introduction to the Theology of St. Thomas Aquinas* (Notre Dame, IN: University of Notre Dame Press, 2002), 57.

13. Joseph Dunne, *Back to the Rough Ground*, 235.

14. Ibid., 319.

15. Josef Pieper, *The Four Cardinal Virtues: Prudence*, trans. Richard Winston and Clara Winston (Notre Dame, IN: University of Notre Dame Press, 1966), 22.

16. Dunne, *Back to the Rough Ground*, 358.

17. Stone, *Evangelism after Christendom*, 33–34.

18. Craig Dykstra, *Growing in the Life of Faith: Education in Christian Practices*, 2nd ed. (Louisville: Westminster/John Knox, 2005), 53–83.

19. Ibid., 76–77; Dykstra, "Reconceiving Practice in Theological Inquiry and Education," in *Virtues and Practices in the Christian Tradition: Christian Ethics after MacIntyre*, ed. Nancy Murphy, Brad J. Kallenberg, and Mark Thiessen Nation (Harrisburg, PA: Trinity, 1997), 164–73.

20. Dunne, *Back to the Rough Ground*, 358–59.

21. Ibid., 361.

22. Michael S. Sherwin, *By Knowledge and By Love: Charity and Morality in the Moral Theology of St. Thomas Aquinas* (Washington, DC: Catholic University of America Press, 2005), 102.

23. Ibid., 106–18.

24. Pinckaers, "Conscience and Christian Tradition," in *The Pinckaers Reader*, 332–33.

25. John Mahoney, S.J., *Seeking the Spirit: Essays in Moral and Pastoral Theology* (London: Sheed & Ward; Denville, NJ: Dimension, 1982), 67–69.

26. Gerald Loughlin, "The Basis and Authority of Doctrine," in *The Cambridge Companion to Christian Doctrine*, ed. Colin E. Gunton (Cambridge: Cambridge University Press, 1997), 57.

27. Aidan Nichols, O.P., *Discovering Aquinas: An Introduction to His Life, Work, and Influence* (Grand Rapids, MI: Eerdmans, 2002), 106.

28. David F. Ford, *Christian Wisdom: Desiring God and Learning in Love* (Cambridge: Cambridge University Press, 2007), 7.

29. Stanley Hauerwas and James Fodor, "Performing Faith," in *Performing the Faith: Bonhoeffer and the Practice of Nonviolence* (Grand Rapids, MI: Brazos, 2004), 81.

30. Romanus Cessario, O.P., *The Virtues, Or the Examined Life* (London and New York: Continuum, 2002), 99–121.

31. Ibid., 114.

32. Fergus Kerr, O.P., *After Aquinas: Versions of Thomism* (London: Blackwell, 2002), 123.

33. Pinckaers, "Conscience and Christian Tradition," in *The Pinckaers Reader*, 332–33.

34. Hauerwas and Fodor, "Performing Faith," 82.

35. Marie-Dominic Chenu, O.P., *Aquinas and His Role in Theology*, trans. Paul Philibert, O.P. (Collegeville, MN: Liturgical, 2002), 111.

36. *Summa Theologica*, I. II q. 66. art 5. resp.1.

37. Herbert McCabe, *The Good Life: Ethics and the Pursuit of Happiness*, ed. Brian Davies, O.P. (London and New York: Continuum, 2005), 91.

38. Pinckaers, "Conscience and Christian Tradition," in *The Pinckaers Reader*, 333–34.

39. Thomas S. Hibbs, *Virtue's Splendor: Wisdom, Prudence, and the Human Good* (New York: Fordham University Press, 2001), 188–89.

40. Wesley, "Address to the Clergy," 485, 499.

41. Ibid., 374.

42. *Works*, 1:405.

43. For the following description I am drawing from *The Works of John Wesley*, 3rd ed., repr. (Grand Rapids, MI: Baker, 1978), 11, 486–92.

44. Ibid., 488–90.

45. Ibid., 490.

46. Ibid., 489.

47. Ibid., 491.

48. Ibid., 486, 492.

49. *Works*, 2:37–38.

50. Daniel W. Hardy and David F. Ford, *Praising and Knowing God* (Philadelphia: Westminster, 1985), 148–52; see the discussion of Wesley, worship, and Methodism in "Worship, Evangelism, Ethics: On Eliminating the 'And,'" in Stanley Hauerwas, *A Better Hope: Resources for a Church Confronting Capitalism, Democracy, and Postmodernity* (Grand Rapids, MI: Brazos, 2000), 155–62; Horton Davies, *Worship and Theology in England, vol. 2: From Watts and Wesley to Martineau, 1690–1900* (Grand Rapids, MI: Eerdmans, 1996), 184–209.

51. See the sermons "On the Trinity" and "The New Creation" in *The Works of John Wesley*, 2:373–86, 500–10; on Wesley and Christian conversion see William H. Willimon, "Suddenly a Light from Heaven" in *Conversion and the Wesleyan Tradition*, ed. Kenneth J. Collins and John H. Tyson (Nashville: Abingdon, 2001).

52. Cf. Randy L. Maddox, *Responsible Grace: John Wesley's Practical Theology* (Nashville: Kingswood Books, 1994), 26–47.

53. Long, *John Wesley's Moral Theology*, 171–202.

54. *Works*, 2:318.

55. "An Address to the Clergy," 484.

56. Ibid., 499.

2. Learning and Devotion

1. Alisdair MacIntyre, *Three Rival Versions of Moral Enquiry: Encyclopedia, Genealogy, and Tradition* (South Bend, IN: University of Notre Dame Press, 1990).

2. Jaroslav Pelikan, *The Vindication of Tradition* (New Haven, CT and London: Yale University Press, 1984), 65. This chapter contains revised material from my *Sacred Rhetoric: Preaching as a Theological and Pastoral Practice* (Grand Rapids, MI: Eerdmans, 2005).

3. Randy L. Maddox, "The Enriching Role of Experience," in *Wesley and the Quadrilateral: Renewing the Conversation* (Nashville: Abingdon, 1997), 125.

4. "An Address to the Clergy," in *The Works of John Wesley*, 3rd ed., repr. (Grand Rapids, MI: Baker, 1978), 488.

5. Paul Holmer, *The Grammar of Faith* (San Francisco, Harper & Row, 1978), 204.

6. Andrew Louth, *Discerning the Mystery: An Essay on the Nature of Theology* (Oxford: Clarendon, 1983), 2–5.

7. Holmer, *The Grammar of Faith*, 203–4.

8. Jeremy Gregory, "The Making of a Protestant Nation: 'Success' and 'Failure' in England's Long Reformation," in *England's Long Reformation 1500–1800*, ed. Nicholas Tyacke (London: UCL, 1998).

9. Albert Outler, *The Wesleyan Theological Heritage: Essays of Albert C. Outler* (Grand Rapids, MI: Zondervan, 1991), 101.

10. Jason E. Vickers, *Invocation and Assent: The Making and Remaking of Trinitarian Theology* (Grand Rapids, MI: Eerdmans, 2008), 37–38.

11. Gary Dorrien, *The Remaking of Evangelical Theology* (Louisville: Westminster/John Knox, 1998), 165–67.

12. *Works*, 3:586.

13. Horton Davies, *Worship and Theology in England: From Watts and Wesley to Martineau, 1690–1900* (Grand Rapids, MI: Eerdmans, 1996), 194–209.

14. Outler, introduction to *Works*, 1:56; Outler, *The Wesleyan Theological Heritage*, 86, 101, 118, 199, 200.

15. A. G. Dickens and Norman Jones suggest that during the later 1510s the *Novum Instrumentum* of Erasmus rather than Luther would have commanded attention at the White Horse Inn. A. G. Dickens and Whitney Jones, *Erasmus the Reformer* (London: Methuen, 1994), 206; James McConica, *English Humanists and Reformation Politics* under Henry VIII and Edward VI (Oxford: Clarendon, 1965), 13–43, 76–105; for comments on notable graduates of late medieval Cambridge, see H. C. Porter, *Reformation and Reaction in Tudor Cambridge* (Cambridge: Cambridge University Press, 1991), 3–20, 41–73; Alec Ryrie, *The Gospel and Henry VIII: Evangelicalism in the Early English Reform* (Cambridge: Cambridge University Press, 2003).

16. Richard J. Schoeck, "Humanism beyond Italy," in *Renaissance Humanism: Foundations, Forms, and Legacy* 3 vols., ed. Albert Rabil Jr. (Philadelphia: University of Pennsylvania Press, 1988), 2.12; I am indebted to Susan R. Wabuda's excellent discussion of Erasmus' work and influence in England, *Preaching during the English Reformation* (Cambridge: Cambridge University Press, 2003), 65–99.

17. Horton Davies, *Worship and Theology in England: From Cranmer to Hooker, 1534–1603* (Princeton, NJ: Princeton University Press, 1970), 2.227–54; Richard Rex, *Henry VIII and the English Reformation* (Oxford and New York: Oxford University Press, 1993), 76–78, 124–26; Lucy E. C. Wooding, *Rethinking Catholicism in Reformation England* (Oxford: Oxford University Press, 2000), 16–48; Wabuda, *Preaching during the English Reformation*, 117–19.

18. Gregory D. Dodds, *Exploiting Erasmus: The Erasmian Legacy and Religious Change in Early Modern England* (Toronto: University of Toronto Press, 2009).

19. Malcolm Underwood, "John Fisher and the Promotion of Learning," in *Humanism, Reform and the Reformation*, ed. Brendan Bradshaw and Eamon Duffy (Cambridge: Cambridge University Press, 1989), 25–46; Richard Rex, *The Theology of John Fisher* (Cambridge: Cambridge University Press, 1991), 50–64.

20. Portions of the material in this section are revised from Michael Pasquarello III, *God's Ploughman, Hugh Latimer: A "Preaching Life"* (Carlisle: Paternoster, forthcoming), chapter 1.

For discussion of shifts in interpretations of Erasmus, see Hilmar M. Pabel, *Conversing with God: Prayer in Erasmus' Pastoral Writings* (Toronto: University of Toronto Press, 1997), 1–10; Pabel, "Promoting the Business of the Gospel: Erasmus' Contribution to Pastoral Ministry," in *ERSY* 15 (1995): 53–70; Manfred Hoffman, *Rhetoric and Theology: The Hermeneutic of Erasmus* (Toronto: University of Toronto Press, 1994), 15–26; Hoffman, "Erasmus on Church and Ministry," in *ERSY* 6 (1986): 1–30; John O'Malley, ed., introduction to *Spiritualia, The Collected Works of Erasmus*

(Toronto and Buffalo: Toronto University Press, 1988–), 66, ix–xxx; Cornelius Augustijn, *Erasmus: His Life, Works, and Influence*, trans. J. C. Grayson (Toronto: University of Toronto Press, 1986), 185–200; Leon-E. Halkin, *Erasmus: A Critical Biography*, trans. John Tonkin (Oxford, UK and Cambridge, Mass: Oxford University Press, 1987), 289–96.

21. Pabel, *Conversing with God*, 4–5.

22. O'Malley, introduction to *CWE* 66:xvii.

23. *CWE* 3:221–22.

24. Hoffman, *Rhetoric and Theology*, 268; see the excellent discussion in Wabuda, *Preaching during the English Reformation*, 64–80; John O'Malley, "Form, Content and Influence of Works about Preaching before Trent: The Franciscan Contribution," chapter 4 in *Religious Culture in the Sixteenth Century: Preaching, Rhetoric, Spirituality and Reform* (New York: Aldershot, 1993).

25. Manfred Hoffman, "Erasmus on Church and Ministry," in *ERSY* 6 (1986): 18–25.

26. Eugene F. Rice Jr., *Saint Jerome and the Renaissance* (Baltimore, MD: Johns Hopkins University Press, 1985), 93–94.

27. Rowan A. Greer, *Broken Lights and Mended Lives: Theology and Common Life in the Early Church* (University Park: Pennsylvania State University Press, 1986), 1–20.

28. Ibid., 12.

29. Eugene Rice Jr., *Saint Jerome and the Renaissance*, 93–94; see the excellent discussion of Erasmus' use of biblical scholarship for training clergy and laity to distinguish faithful and unfaithful pastoral practice in Jane E. Philips, "The Gospel, the Clergy, and the Laity in Erasmus 'Paraphrase on the Gospel of John'" in *ERSY* 10 (1990): 85–100.

30. Pabel, *Conversing with God*, 9.

31. O'Malley, introduction to *CWE* 66:xxx.

32. For a good discussion see Erika Rummel, *The Humanist-Scholastic Debate: In the Renaissance and Reformation* (Cambridge: Cambridge University Press, 1998), 96–125.

33. Cited in Augustijn, *Erasmus*, 103.

34. *CWE* 3:204, 222.

35. R. J. Schoeck, *Erasmus of Europe: The Making of a Humanist: 1500–1536* (Edinburgh: T&T Clark, 1992), 190.

36. Marjoire O'Rourke Boyle, *Erasmus on Language and Method in Theology* (Toronto and Buffalo: University of Toronto Press, 1977), 1–57; Hoffman, *Rhetoric and Theology*, 81–93.

37. Hoffman, "Erasmus on Church and Ministry," 27.

38. Desiderius Erasmus, *The Paraclesis*, in *Christian Humanism and the Reformation: Selected Writings of Erasmus*, ed. John Olin, 3rd ed. (New York: Fordham University Press, 1987), 97–108.

39. Augustijn, *Erasmus*, 78–79; O'Malley, CWE 66:xxvi.

40. Dickens and Jones, *Erasmus the Reformer*, 198; see the assessment of Margaret Mann Phillips, *Erasmus and the Northern Renaissance* (New York: Collier, 1965). "Almost all the ideas expressed in the *Paraclesis* were in accordance with those expressed by Luther" (85).

41. Erasmus, *Paraclesis*, 98–99.

42. Ibid., 98.

43. Marjorie O'Rourke Boyle, "Rhetorical Theology: Charity Seeking Charity," in *Rhetorical Invention and Religious Inquiry: New Perspectives*, ed. Walter Jost and Wendy Olmstead (New Haven, CT and London: Yale University Press, 2000), 88–89.

44. Martha C. Nussbaum, *The Therapy of Desire: Theory and Practice in Hellenistic Ethics* (Princeton, NJ: Princeton University Press, 1994), 3–7; Piere Hadot, *Philosophy as a Way of Life: Spiritual Exercises from Socrates to Foucault*, ed. Arnold I. Davidson, trans. Michael Chase (Oxford: Oxford University Press,1995), 47–144; John T. McNeill, *A History of the Cure of Souls* (New York: Harper, 1951), 17–41.

45. Erasmus, *Paraclesis*, 99.

46. Jaroslav Pelikan, *Christianity and Classical Culture: The Metamorphosis of Natural Theology in the Christian Encounter with Hellenism* (New Haven and London: Yale University Press, 1993), 178–80.

47. Manfred Hoffman, "Faith and Piety in Erasmus' Thought," in *Sixteenth Century Journal* 20.2 (1998): 248.

48. Erasmus, *Paraclesis*, 100.

49. Hoffman, "Faith and Piety in Erasmus' Thought," 248.

50. Ibid., 249.

51. Erasmus, *Paraclesis*, 101: "So the humanist effort was not restricted to scholarly pursuits and the world of intellectual elites. Its clear objective was the education and salvation of simple folk, and this aim was to unleash a flood of vernacular literature"; Wooding, *Rethinking Catholicism*, 22.

52. Erasmus, *Paraclesis*, 102.

53. Hoffman, *Rhetoric and Theology*, 61; R. J. Schoeck, *Erasmus Grandescens: The Growth of a Humanist's Mind* (Nieuwkoop: DeGraaf, 1988), 83–84; Rex, *The Theology of John Fisher*, 60–61; Boyle, *Erasmus on Language and Method in Theology*, 100–101.

54. Erasmus, *Paraclesis*, 102.

55. Ibid., 102–3; for a discussion of Erasmus' critique of late medieval piety and its reliance on images, see Carlos M. N. Erie, *War against the Idols: The Reformation of*

Worship from Erasmus to Calvin (Cambridge: Cambridge University Press, 1996), 36–45. "Erasmus, in the first place, considered religious images as powerless . . . the Christian ought to revere the portrait of God's mind that the skill of the Holy Spirit has portrayed in the writing of the Gospels," 39. On Erasmus' view of history and human responsibility for the past, see Istvan Bejczy, *Erasmus and the Middle Ages: The Historical Consciousness of a Christian Humanist* (Leiden: Brill, 2001), 182–90.

56. Hoffman, *Rhetoric and Theology*, 62.

57. See Debora Shuger's discussion of the emphasis placed by Renaissance rhetorics on the passion of the preacher's heart and speech being enflamed by divine charity; Shuger, *Sacred Rhetoric: The Christian Grand Style in the English Renaissance* (Princeton: Princeton University Press, 1988), 221–40.

58. Wabuda, *Preaching during the English Reformation*, 69, 65–69; see the discussion in O'Malley, "Erasmus and the History of Sacred Rhetoric" as composed in chapter 4 in *Religious Culture*.

59. Hoffman, "Erasmus on Church and Ministry," 23–25.

60. Ibid., 24.

61. Augustijn, *Erasmus*, 99–102; Albert Rabil Jr., *Erasmus and the New Testament: The Mind of a Christian Humanist* (San Antonio: Trinity, 1972), 115–41.

62. CWE 7:5.

63. CWE 5:196.

64. Mark Vessey, introduction to *Holy Scripture Speaks: The Production and Reception of Erasmus' Paraphrases on the New Testament*, ed. Hilmar Pabel and Mark Vessey (Toronto: University of Toronto Press, 2002), 8.

65. J. J. Bateman, "From Soul to Soul: Persuasion in Erasmus' 'Paraphrases on the New Testament,'" in *Erasmus in English 15* (1987–88): 8.

66. CWE 42:xiv–xviii; Albert Rabil Jr., "Erasmus' Paraphrases on the New Testament," in *Essays on the Works of Erasmus*, ed. Richard DeMolen (New Haven, CT: Yale University Press, 1978), 145–62.

67. In *Erasmus the Reformer*, Jones and Dickens conclude that England was the nation most receptive to Erasmus' philosophy of Christ. See "The English Erasmians," 192–216.

68. On Erasmus' rhetorical reading of Scripture and the relation of human and divine discourse see Debora Shuger, *The Renaissance Bible: Scholarship, Sacrifice, and Subjectivity* (Berkeley and Los Angeles: University of California Press, 1998), 25–26; Shuger, *Sacred Rhetoric*, 243–49.

69. *CWE* 41:x–xii; Bateman, "From Soul to Soul: Persuasion in Erasmus' Paraphrases on the New Testament," 7–16.

70. *CWE* 44:103.

71. On the importance of Augustine for sacred rhetoric in the sixteenth century see Shuger, *Sacred Rhetoric*, 47–65; for a discussion of Erasmus and his use of Augustine see Peter Iver Kaufman, *Augustinian Piety and Catholic Reform: Augustine, Colet, and Erasmus* (Macon, GA: Mercer University Press, 1982), 111–28; James McConica, *Erasmus* (Oxford and New York: Oxford University Press, 1991), 14, 15; on the rhetorical theology of Erasmus see O'Malley, introduction to *CWE* 66:xxviii–xxvix; Charles Trinkaus, *In Our Image and Likeness*, 2 vols. (Chicago: University of Chicago Press, 1970), 1.126–28; John D' Amico, "Humanism and Pre-Reformation Theology," in *Renaissance Humanism: Foundations, Forms, and Legacy*, 3 vols., ed. Albert Rabil Jr., (Philadelphia: University of Pennsylvania Press, 1988), 3.369–73.

72. Wabuda, *Preaching during the English Reformation*, 69.

73. Dodds, *Exploiting Erasmus*, 27–59.

74. "An Address to the Clergy," 487–88, 491.

75. Ibid., 488–89.

76. Ibid., 498.

77. Ibid., 486–87.

3. Back to the Future

1. *The Bicentennial Edition of the Works of John Wesley*, ed. Albert C. Outler (Nashville: Abingdon, 1984–), 3:581–82. Hereafter referred to as *Works*.

2. Frank Baker, *John Wesley and the Church of England* (Nashville: Abingdon, 1970).

3. Kenneth J. Collins, *A Faithful Witness: John Wesley's Homiletical Theology* (Wilmore, KY: Wesley Heritage, 1993).

4. Cited in *Certain Sermons or Homilies (1547) And a Homily against Disobedience and Wilful Rebellion (1570)*, ed. Ronald B. Bond (Toronto: University of Toronto Press, 1987), 15–16.

5. *John Wesley*, ed. Albert C. Outler (New York: Oxford University Press, 1964), 121–33.

6. Cited in Albert Outler, *The Wesleyan Theological Heritage: Essays of Albert C. Outler*, ed. Thomas C. Oden and Leicester R. Longden (Grand Rapids, MI: Zondervan, 1991), 66.

7. *The Journal of the Reverend John Wesley, A.M.*, ed. Nehemiah Curnock (London: Epworth, 1960–), 2.101.

8. Horton Davies, *Worship and Theology in England: From Watts to Wesley to Martineau, 1690–1900* (Grand Rapids, MI: Eerdmans, 1996), 2.194–97.

9. William J. Abraham, *Wesley for Armchair Theologians* (Louisville: Westminster/John Knox, 2005), 28.

10. Outler, *The Wesleyan Theological Heritage*, 35.

11. Jason E. Vickers, *Wesley: A Guide for the Perplexed* (London and New York: T&T Clark, 2009), 35.

12. Ibid., 40–43.

13. D. Stephen Long, *John Wesley's Moral Theology: The Quest for God and Goodness* (Nashville: Abingdon, 2005), 2.

14. Bryan Stone, *Evangelism after Christendom: The Theology and Practice of Christian Witness* (Grand Rapids, MI: Brazos, 2007), 11.

15. Vickers, *Wesley*, 28–31.

16. Outler, *The Wesleyan Theological Heritage*, 46.

17. Cited in Robert E. Cushman, *John Wesley's Experimental Divinity: Studies in Methodist Doctrinal Standards* (Nashville: Abingdon, 1989), 40.

18. Cf. Susan Wabuda, *Preaching during the English Reformation* (Cambridge and New York: Cambridge University Press, 2002); Peter E. McCullough, *Sermons at Court: Politics and Religion in Elizabethan and Jacobean Preaching* (Cambridge: Cambridge University Press, 1998), 51–59; R. N. Swanson, *Church and Society in Late Medieval England* (Oxford: Clarendon, 1989), 347–61; G. W. Blench, *Preaching in England* (Oxford: Oxford University Press, 1964), 87–94.

19. *Certain Sermons or Homilies*, ed. Ronald B. Bond (Toronto: University of Toronto Press, 1987).

20. Patrick Collinson, *The Birthpangs of Protestant England: Religious and Cultural Change in the Sixteenth and Seventeenth Centuries* (New York: St. Martin's, 1988), 1–11; Peter Marshall, *The Catholic Priesthood and the English Reformation* (Oxford: Clarendon, 1994), 86–107.

21. John N. Wall, "Godly and Fruitful Lessons: The English Bible, Erasmus' Paraphrases, and the Book of Homilies," in *The Godly Kingdom of Tudor England: Great Books of the English Reformation*, ed. John Booty (Wilton, CT: Morehouse-Barlow, 1981), 47–138; John N. King, *English Reformation Literature* (Princeton, NJ: Princeton University Press, 1985), 122–30. For my understanding of the background, content, and purpose of the *Book of Homilies*, I am indebted to the work of John N. Wall, "The Vision of a Christian Commonwealth in the *Book of Homilies* (PhD diss., Harvard University, 1979).

22. John N. Wall, *Transformations of the Word: Spenser, Herbert, and Vaughn* (Athens: University of Georgia Press, 1988), 1–34.

23. Wall, "Godly and Fruitful Lessons," 47–58; Wabuda, *Preaching during the English Reformation*, 144–45.

24. *Homilies*, 3–6; Wabuda, *Preaching during the English Reformation*, 144–45.

25. "The Edwardian Injunctions, 1547," in *Documents of the English Reformation*, ed. Gerald Bray, (Minneapolis, MN: Augsburg, 1994), 256.

26. *Homilies*, 6–7; on the regulative function of doctrine as grammar see George Lindbeck, *The Nature of Doctrine: Religion and Theology in a Postliberal Age* (Philadelphia: Westminster, 1984), 91–107; on the need for Protestants to develop regulative norms for biblical interpretation in the sixteenth century see David C. Steinmetz, *Luther in Context* (Bloomington: Indiana University Press, 1986), 86–91.

27. Susan Brigden, *London and the Reformation* (Oxford: Clarendon, 1989), 442–43.

28. Diarmaid MacCulloch, *Tudor Church Militant: Edward VI and the Protestant Reformation* (London: Allen Lane, 1999), 12.

29. Nicholas Ridley, *Works*, ed. H. Christmas (Cambridge: Cambridge University Press, 1851), 400.

30. King, *English Reformation Literature*, 123–27; these views echo those set forth by Desiderius Erasmus. See Erasmus, *The Paraclesis*, in *Christian Humanism and the Reformation: Selected Writings of Erasmus*, ed. John C. Olin, 3rd ed. (New York: Fordham University, 1987), 97–108.

31. Wall, "Godly and Fruitful Lessons," 90–93.

32. King, *English Reformation Literature*, 152–60; Margaret Aston, *England's Iconoclasts: Laws against Images* (Oxford: Oxford University Press, 1988), 1.125–36.

33. Bond, *Certain Sermons or Homilies*, 3; Wall, "Godly and Fruitful Lessons," 95–103.

34. Wall, "Godly and Fruitful Lessons," 124–25; *Homilies*, 62.

35. *Homilies*, 66–67.

36. Robert E. Cushman, *John Wesley's Experimental Divinity: Studies in Methodist Doctrinal Standards* (Nashville: Kingswood Books, 1989), 11.

37. John Wesley, "The Doctrine of Salvation, Faith and Good Works, Extracted from the Homilies of the Church of England," ed. Albert C. Outler (New York: Oxford University Press, 1964), 127.

38. Ibid., 130.

39. Ibid., 131–32.

40. Cushman, *John Wesley's Experimental Divinity*, 46.

41. Ibid., 10–11.

42. Ibid., 20–21.

43. *Works*, 1:106.

44. *Works*, "The Means of Grace," 378.

45. Ibid., 378–79.

46. D. Stephen Long, *John Wesley's Moral Theology: The Quest for God and Goodness* (Nashville: Abingdon, 2005), 154.

47. *Works*, 1:382–83.

48. Ibid., 1:383.

49. Ibid., 1:383–84.

50. Ibid., 1:387–88.

51. Ibid., 1:393–94.

52. Ibid., 1:394–95.

53. Ibid., 1:396.

54. Ibid., 1:377.

55. Ibid., 1:397.

56. *Sermons, or Homilies, Appointed to Be Read in Churches in the Time of Queen Elizabeth, of Famous Memory* (London: The Prayer Book and Homily Society, 1817), 1–3.

4. Speaking the Truth in Love

1. *The Bicentennial Edition of the Works of John Wesley*, ed. Albert C. Outler (Nashville: Abingdon, 1984–), 1:103–4. Hereafter referred to as *Works*.

2. Introduction to *Works*, 1:28–29.

3. D. Stephen Long, *John Wesley's Moral Theology: The Quest for God and Goodness* (Nashville: Abingdon, 2005), 118–19.

4. Horton Davies, *Worship and Theology in England: From Watts and Wesley to Martineau, 1690–1900* (Grand Rapids, MI: Eerdmans, 1996), 143–83.

5. E. Brooks Holifield, *Theology in America: Christian Thought from the Age of the Puritans to the Civil War* (New Haven, CT and London: Yale University Press, 2003), 260.

6. Mark A. Noll, *America's God: From Jonathan Edwards to Abraham Lincoln* (Oxford: Oxford University Press, 2002), 188–95; in this section I am also following Mark A. Noll, *The Rise of Evangelicalism: The Age of Edwards, Whitefield and the Wesleys* (Downers Grove, IL: InterVarsity, 2003); Nathan O. Hatch, *The Democratization of American Christianity* (New Haven, CT: Yale University Press, 1989); *The Bible in America: Essays in Cultural History*, ed. Mark A. Noll and Nathan O. Hatch (Oxford: Oxford University Press, 1982); Jon Butler, *Awash in a Sea of Faith: Christianizing the American People* (Cambridge, MA: Harvard University Press, 1990); William G. McLoughlin, *Modern Revivalism: Charles Grandison Finney to Billy Graham* (New York: Ronald Press, 1959); George M. Marsden, *Reforming Fundamentalism: Fuller Seminary and the New Evangelicalism* (Grand Rapids, MI: Eerdmans, 1987); E. Brooks Holifield, *Theology in America: Christian Thought from the Age of the Puritans to the Civil War* (New Haven, CT and London: Yale University Press, 2003).

7. Noll, *America's God*, 190; Hatch, *The Democratization of American Christianity*, 197–200.

8. Noll, *The Rise of Evangelicalism,* 270–78, 290; Holifield, *Theology in America,* 361–68.

9. Cited in Noll, *America's God,* 236.

10. Noll, *America's God,* 380–83; Hatch, *The Democratization of American Christianity,* 182–83.

11. Hughes Oliphant Old, *The Reading and Preaching of the Scriptures in the Worship of the Christian Church: The Modern Age* (Grand Rapids, MI: Eerdmans, 2007), 6.579–80.

12. Timothy P. Weber, "Revivals," in *Concise Encyclopedia of Preaching,* ed. William H. Willimon and Richard Lischer (Louisville: Westminster/John Knox, 1995), 407.

13. Rodney Clapp, *Border Crossings: Christian Trespasses on Popular Culture and Public Affairs* (Grand Rapids, MI: Brazos, 2000), 136–45.

14. William H. Willimon, *The Intrusive Word: Preaching to the Unbaptized* (Grand Rapids, MI: Eerdmans, 1994), 15–26; for a good discussion of evangelistic strategies among seeker-sensitive churches see Todd E. Johnson, "Truth Decay: Rethinking Evangelism in the New Century," in *The Strange New Word of the Gospel: Re-evangelizing in the Postmodern World,* ed. Carl E. Bratten and Robert W. Johnson (Grand Rapids, MI: Eerdmans, 2002), 118–39.

15. James F. Kay, *Preaching and Theology* (St. Louis: Chalice, 2007), 49–50.

16. I am indebted here to Philip Kenneson, "Selling (Out) the Church in the Marketplace of Desire," *Modern Theology* 9:4 (October 1993): 1–25.

17. See the excellent critique and analysis of contemporary evangelism in Bryan Stone, *Evangelism after Christendom: The Theology and Practice of Christian Witness* (Grand Rapids, MI: Brazos, 2007), 23–54.

18. Quoted by Outler in introduction to *Works,* 1:25.

19. *Works,* 1:103.

20. "The Unity of the Divine Being," *Works,* 4:67.

21. Long, *John Wesley's Moral Theology,* 15–16.

22. On the relation between trinitarian doctrine and moral judgment see L. Gregory Jones, *Transformed Judgment: Toward a Trinitarian Account of the Moral Life* (Notre Dame, IN: University of Notre Dame Press, 1990).

23. Long, *John Wesley's Moral Theology,* 142–43.

24. Ibid., 82–83.

25. Ibid., 54–55.

26. Ibid., 69.

27. Cited in ibid., 119.

28. Christopher Haigh, *English Reformations: Religion, Politics, and Society under the Tudors* (Oxford: Clarendon, 1993), 189; Jeremy Gregory suggests we see the English

Reformation as a revival as well as a reform, that it aimed to both purge and bring to life the old faith in a new form appropriate for its future; see his "The Making of a Protestant Nation," in *England's Long Reformation 1500–1800*, ed. Nicholas Tyacke (London: Ashgate, 1998), 314–20; for a good description of the Edwardians' emphasis on preaching, see Catharine Davies, *A Religion of the Word: The Defence of the Reformation in the Reign of Edward VI* (Manchester, UK: Manchester University Press, 2002), 87–93; Haigh, *English Reformations*, 189–202; Robert Whiting, *Local Responses to the English Reformation* (New York: St. Martin's, 1998), 167–82; Christopher Marsh, *Popular Religion in Sixteenth Century England: Holding Their Peace* (New York: St. Martin's, 1998), 32–42, 52–54, 119–22; Robert Whiting, *The Blind Devotion of the People: Popular Religion and the English Reformation* (Cambridge and New York: Cambridge University Press, 1989), 234–55; Nicholas Tyacke, "Introduction: Re-Thinking the 'English Reformation,' " in *England's Long Reformation 1500–1800*, 4–7.

29. David Steinmetz, "The Intellectual Appeal of the Reformation," in *Theology Today* 57:4 (2001): 460–61.

30. "There was probably no other single aspect of the Reformation in England that touched more directly and fundamentally the consciousness, or lack of it, of ordinary clergy and laity, than did the reform of rituals and liturgy" (Judith Maltby, *Prayer Book and People in Elizabethan and Early Stuart England* [Cambridge: Cambridge University Press, 1998], 4); see the conclusions drawn by Sharon Arnoult, "Spiritual and Sacred Publique Actions: The Book of Common Prayer and the Understanding of Worship in the Elizabethan and Jacobean Church of England," in *Religion and the English People 1500–1640: New Voices, New Perspectives*, ed. Eric Josef Carlson, *Sixteenth Century Essays and Studies* 45 (Kirksville, MO: Thomas Jefferson University Press, 1998): 25–48.

31. John Wall, *Transformations of the Word: Spenser, Herbert, and Vaughn* (Athens: University of Georgia Press, 1988), 11–15.

32. *Documents of the English Reformation*, ed. G. Bray (Minneapolis, MN: Augsburg, 1994), 273; MacCulloch uses the term *reformed Catholic* to describe the position of Cranmer, which also could apply to Latimer: "for they [the reformers] sought to build up the Catholic Church on the same foundations of Bible, creeds, and the great councils of the early Church . . . Cranmer was guiding the Church of England to a renewed Catholicity through thickets of wicked deceit which must be avoided at all costs; on the one hand, papistry, and on the other Anabaptism, both equally 'sects' in his eyes." See Diarmaid MacCulloch, *Thomas Cranmer: A Life* (New Haven, CT: Yale University Press, 1996), 617; Paul Avis, *Anglicanism and the Christian Church: Theological Resources in Historical Perspective* (London and New York: T&T Clark, 2002): "Particular (i.e., national) churches are catholic when they profess and teach

the faith and religion of Christ according to the scripture and apostolic doctrine" (35).

33. Marsh, *Popular Religion in Sixteenth-Century England*, 195–216; see the essay by Eric Josef Carlson, "New Research on Religion in Tudor and Early Stuart England," in *Religion and the English People 1500–1640: New Voices, New Perspectives*, ed. Eric Josef Carlson (Kirksville, MO: Thomas Jefferson University Press, 1988), 3. "If the English Reformation is seen as sort of a dialectical process in which a synthesis was shaped over time, things start to make sense."

34. Marsh, *Popular Religion in Sixteenth-Century England*, 197–20; Jeremy, "The Making of a Protestant Nation," 314–33.

35. Marsh, *Popular Religion in Sixteenth-Century England*, 206–7; Frank Senn, "The Reform of the Mass," in *The Catholicity of the Reformation*, ed. Carl Bratten and Robert W. Jenson (Grand Rapids, MI: Eerdmans, 1996), 47–50. On Cranmer's moderating position, Senn states: "It seemed, however, that no one was satisfied with the prayer book." For a detailed account of Cranmer's struggle over acceptance of the prayer book with Hooper on one hand and Gardiner on the other, and his attempt to secure the cooperation of both, see MacCulloch, *Thomas Cranmer*, 454–93.

36. Wall, *Transformations of the Word*, 47.

37. Bray, *Documents of the English Reformation*, 273.

38. John N. King, *English Reformation Literature: The Tudor Origins of the Protestant Tradition* (Princeton, NJ: Princeton University Press, 1982), 135–36.

39. Bray, *Documents of the English Reformation*, 281.

40. George Blench, *Preaching in England* (Oxford: Oxford University Press, 1964), 142–53; Harold S. Darby, *Hugh Latimer* (London: Epworth, 1953), 201–55; John Tulloch, *Luther and Other Leaders of the Reformation* (Edinburgh: W. Blackwood, 1883), 339–51; Robert Demaus, *Hugh Latimer: A Biography* (Nashville: Lamar and Barton, 1903), 468–71; Charles Smyth, *The Art of Preaching: A Practical Survey of Preaching in the Church of England 747–1939* (London: SPCK; New York: MacMillan, 1940), 107.

41. Smyth, *The Art of Preaching in the Church of England*, 107; Davies, *Worship and Theology in England*, "Latimer was a people's preacher, not a preacher's preacher" (1:248); see G. R. Owst's description of medieval popular preaching, *Preaching in Medieval England* (Cambridge: Cambridge University Press, 1926), 253–333.

42. See Shuger, *Sacred Rhetoric*, 243–44: "In England, the vernacular sacred rhetorics tend to carry on the medieval passionate plain style under Protestant auspices."

43. H. O. Taylor, *Thought and Expression in the Sixteenth Century* (New York, 1925), 125.

44. Bray, *Documents of the English Reformation*, 238–39.

45. Desiderius Erasmus, *The Praise of Folly*, trans. and ed. Clarence H. Miller (New Haven, CT: Yale University Press, 1979), 101; see also Blench, *Preaching in England*, 113–41; G. R. Owst, *Literature and Pulpit in Medieval England* (Cambridge: Cambridge University Press, 1933), 210–86; Janet L. Mueller, *The Native Tongue and the Word: Developments in English Prose Style 1380–1580* (Chicago: University of Chicago Press, 1984), 164–72. Mueller shows that aureation and authority were joined in Latinity to grant late medieval clergy power over the laity. Preaching and writing in the vernacular gave the Reformers the advantage of immediate, personal, oral communication. Their scripturalism, based on the imitation of the Bible, and their modest use of rhetoric, as derived from and subordinated to Scripture's message, gave preaching a freshness and directness that was not typical of late medieval learned clergy; see the discussion by King, *English Reformation Literature*, 122–44.

46. Shuger, *Sacred Rhetoric*, 151–218.

47. *The Works of Saint Augustine: A Translation for the 21st Century, Teaching Christianity:* De Doctrina Christiana, 1/11, John E. Rotelle, O.S.A. ed. (Hyde Park, NY: New City, 1996), IV.31.64. Hereafter references will be included within the text, *DDC*. For a good introduction to Augustine's pastoral theology see Mark Ellingsen, *The Richness of Augustine: His Contextual and Pastoral Theology* (Louisville: Westminster/John Knox, 2005). For a good introduction to pastoral theology that unites doctrine and practice see Andrew Purves, *Reconstructing Pastoral Theology: A Christological Foundation* (Louisville: Westminster/John Knox, 2005).

48. For interpretations of *De doctrina christiana* see Duane W. H. Arnold and Pamela Bright, ed., *De Doctrina Christiana: A Classic of Western Culture* (Notre Dame, IN: University of Notre Dame Press, 1996); and Carol Harrison, *Augustine: Christian Truth and Fractured Humanity* (Oxford: Oxford University Press, 2000), chaps. 2–3; see also the comments on the church in Oliver Davies, *A Theology of Compassion: Metaphysics of Difference and the Renewal of Tradition* (London: SCM, 2001), 274–76; see the integrative, theological interpretation of *DDC* in David Tracy, "Charity, Obscurity, and Clarity: Augustine's Search for Rhetoric and Hermeneutics," in *Rhetoric and Hermeneutics in Our Time*, ed. Walter Jost and Michael J. Hyde (New Haven, CT and London: Yale University Press, 1997), 254–74; for a more comprehensive study I am indebted to William Harmless, *Augustine and the Catechumenate* (Collegeville, MN: Liturgical, 1995).

49. Telford Work, *Living and Active: Scripture in the Economy of Salvation* (Grand Rapids, MI: Eerdmans, 2001), 59–60.

50. Davies, *A Theology of Compassion*, 81.

51. James Patout Burns, "Delighting the Spirit: Augustine's Practice of Figurative Interpretation," in *De Doctrina Christiana*, 189–92.

52. See the discussion in Aidan Nichols, O.P., *The Art of God Incarnate: Theology and Image in Christian Tradition* (London: Darton, Longman & Todd, 1980).

53. Erich Auerbach, *Literary Language and Its Public in Late Antiquity and in the Middle Ages*, trans. Ralph Manheim (New York: Princeton University Press, 1965), 31–66.

54. See King's treatment of Robert Crowley's 1550 edition of *Piers Plowman in English Reformation Literature*, 319–39. In terms of being radical, as in the "root" of the matter, the popular sermons may be more radical in activity if not in tone, simply because they are the actual implementation of the vision articulated in earlier sermons.

55. Auerbach, *Literary Language*, 39–47; see the excellent discussion by Peter Auski, *Christian Plain Style: The Evolution of a Spiritual Ideal* (Montreal: McGill-Queen's University Press, 1995), 13–67, 232–66. The Franciscans also offered a style of *Sermo Humilis* preaching that utilized narrative, emotion and the commonplace, focusing on the humanity of Christ in his incarnation and his passion. Peter Hawkins, *Dante's Testaments: Essays in Scriptural Imagination* (Stanford: Stanford University Press, 1999), 23; on Franciscan preaching see Hugh Oliphant Old, *The Reading and Preaching of the Scripture in the Christian Church: The Medieval Period* (Grand Rapids, MI: Eerdmans, 1998), 3:342–48.

56. Peter Brown, *Power and Persuasion in Late Antiquity* (Madison: University of Wisconsin Press, 1988), 74–76.

57. *John Wesley*, ed. Albert C. Outler, "Doctrines and Discipline in the Minutes of the Annual Conferences, 1744–1747" (New York: Oxford University Press, 1980), 160–61.

5. The Way to God

1. See the discussion of the "tyranny of the practical" and related matters in Bryan P. Stone, *Evangelism after Christendom: The Theology and Practice of Christian Witness* (Grand Rapids, MI: Brazos, 2007).

2. Here I have benefited from the introductory argument in D. Stephen Long, *John Wesley's Moral Theology: The Quest for God and Goodness* (Nashville: Kingswood Books, 2005).

3. *The Bicentennial Edition of the Works of John Wesley*, ed. Albert C. Outler (Nashville: Abingdon, 1984–), 1:517. Hereafter referred to as *Works*.

4. I am indebted to Randy Maddox's use of "practical atheism" as a way of describing visions of Christian life and practice separating God and humanity. Cf. Randy L. Maddox, *Responsible Grace: John Wesley's Practical Theology* (Nashville: Kingswood Books, 1985), 322. In this kind of functioning that follows the logic of marketing and the business world, the mode of delivery does not matter—disc, computer screen, video hookup, cell phone or iPod messaging—so long as delivery occurs.

5. "An Address to the Clergy," *The Works of John Wesley, M.A.*, ed. Thomas Jackson (Grand Rapids, MI: Zondervan, 1958–59), 10:486.

6. *Sermons, or Homilies, Appointed to Be Read in Churches in the Time of Queen Elizabeth of Famous Memory* (London: The Prayer Book and Homily Society, 1817), 4.

7. "An Address to the Clergy," 486.

8. Ibid., 486–87.

9. *Sermons, or Homilies*, 8.

10. See Outler's extensive introductory comments on Wesley's formulations of holiness in *Wesley* (New York: Oxford University Press, 1964), 31.

11. Frank C. Senn, *New Creation: A Liturgical Worldview* (Minneapolis, MN: Augsburg Fortress, 2000), 15–16, 30–35.

12. See the excellent discussion in Rowan Williams, *On Christian Theology* (Oxford, UK and Malden, MA: Blackwell, 2000), 142–48.

13. Robert W. Wall, "Toward a Wesleyan Hermeneutic of Scripture," in *Reading the Bible in Wesleyan Ways: Some Constructive Proposals*, ed. Barry L. Callen and Richard P. Thompson (Kansas City, MO: Beacon Hill, 2004), 54.

14. Here I am indebted to the work of Scott J. Jones, *John Wesley's Conception and Use of Scripture* (Nashville: Abingdon, 1995).

15. "An Address to the Clergy," 493.

16. See the excellent discussion in Charles L. Campbell, *Preaching Jesus: New Directions for Homiletics in Hans Frei's Postliberal Theology* (Grand Rapids, MI: Eerdmans, 1997), 117–88.

17. Hans W. Frei, *The Eclipse of Biblical Narrative: A Study in Eighteenth and Nineteenth Century Hermeneutics* (New Haven, CT and London: Yale University Press, 1974), 153–54.

18. Jason E. Vickers, *Invocation and Assent: The Making and Remaking of Trinitarian Theology* (Grand Rapids, MI: Eerdmans, 2008).

19. Ibid., 169–90. Vickers devotes most of his work to Charles rather than John. My point in this chapter is that John's work also displays a trinitarian rule.

20. Robert E. Cushman, *John Wesley's Experimental Divinity: Studies in Methodist Doctrinal Standards* (Nashville: Abingdon, 1989), 10.

21. *The Wesleyan Theological Heritage: Essays of Albert C. Outler*, ed. Thomas C. Oden and Leicester R. Longden (Grand Rapids, MI: Zondervan, 1991), 104–5; introduction to *Works*, 1:75.

22. For good discussions of Irenaeus see Eric Osborn, *Irenaeus of Lyons* (Cambridge: Cambridge University Press, 2001); Basil Studer, *Trinity and Incarnation: The Faith of the Early Church*, ed. Andrew Louth (Collegeville, MN: Liturgical, 1993); Rowan A. Greer, *Broken Lights and Mended Lives: Theology and Common Life in the Early Church* (University Park: Pennsylvania State University Press, 1986); John Behr, *The Formation of Christian Theology: The Way to Nicea*, vol. 1 (Crestwood, NY: St. Vladimir's Press, 2001); John O'Keefe and R. R. Reno, *Sanctified Vision: An Introduction to Early Christian Interpretation of the Bible* (Baltimore and London: Johns Hopkins University Press, 2005).

23. Rowan Greer, "The Christian Bible and Its Interpretation," in *Early Biblical Interpretation*, ed. Wayne Meeks (Philadelphia: Westminster, 1986), 111.

24. Jeremy Driscoll, O.S.B., "Uncovering the Dynamic *Lex Orandi—Lex Credendi* in the Baptismal Theology of Irenaeus," *Pro Ecclesia* 12:2 (Spring 2003): 214–15.

25. Ibid.; "Uncovering the Dynamic *Lex Orandi—Lex Credendi*," 219.

26. See the excellent introduction in Greer, *Broken Lights and Mended Lives*, 1–20.

27. St. Irenaeus of Lyons, *On the Apostolic Preaching*, trans. John Behr (Crestwood, NY: St. Vladimir's Press, 1997), 39. Hereafter references will appear in the text as Dem.

28. Behr, *Formation of Christian Theology*, 112–13.

29. Driscoll, "Uncovering the Dynamic *Lex Orandi—Lex Credendi*," 218.

30. Ibid., 217.

31. Greer, *Broken Lights and Mended Lights*, 26–27.

32. Robert Louis Wilken, *The Spirit of Early Christian Thought: Seeking the Face of God* (New Haven, CT and London: Yale University Press, 2003), 66–67.

33. Paul Blowers, "The *Regula Fidei* and the Narrative Character of Early Christian Faith," *Pro Ecclesia* 6 (1997): 203–4; see the excellent discussion in Francis Young, *Virtuoso Theology: The Bible and Interpretation* (Cleveland: Pilgrim), 47–65.

34. Behr, *Formation of Christian Theology*, 119–24; Greer, *Broken Lights and Mended Lives*, 26–31.

35. Behr, *Formation of Christian Theology*, 124–26.

36. Greer, *Broken Lights and Mended Lives*, 25–27; Greer, "The Christian Bible and Its Interpretation," 171–76.

37. Greer, *Broken Lights and Mended Lives*, 37.

38. Blowers, "The *Regula Fidei* and the Narrative Character of Early Christian Faith," 203–4.

39. Colin E. Guntion, *The One, The Three and the Many: God, Creation and the Culture of Modernity* (Cambridge: Cambridge University Press, 1993), 225–31; Wilken, *The Spirit of Early Christianity*, 25–49.

40. Robert W. Jenson, "Hermeneutics and the Life of the Church," in *Reclaiming the Bible for the Church*, ed. Carl E. Bratten and Robert W. Jenson (Grand Rapids, MI: Eerdmans, 1995), 98.

41. Rowan Greer (with James Kugel), *Early Biblical Interpretation* (Philadelphia: Westminster/John Knox, 1986), 198–99.

42. "An Address to the Clergy," 498.

43. For Wesley's discussion of the text's authenticity see John Wesley, *Explanatory Notes on the New Testament*, 2 vols. (Peabody, MA: Hendrickson, 1986).

44. *Works*, 2:385.

45. Geoffrey Wainwright, "The Trinitarian Hermeneutic of John Wesley," in *Reading the Bible in Wesleyan Ways*. This essay is particularly helpful for understanding Wesley's theological reading of Scripture.

46. Here I recommend the collection of essays in *Reading the Bible in Wesleyan Ways*.

47. "An Address to the Clergy," 485–86.

48. Peter M. Candler Jr., *Theology, Rhetoric, Manuduction: Or Reading Scripture Together on the Path to God* (Grand Rapids, MI and Cambridge: Eerdmans, 2006), 13–14.

49. Ibid., 16.

50. Matthew Levering, *Participatory Biblical Exegesis: A Theology of Biblical Interpretation* (Notre Dame, IN: University of Notre Dame Press, 2008), 1.

51. Ibid., 14–36.

52. Ibid., 3–7.

53. *Works*, 1:104–5.

54. Ibid. See the comments by Outler in notes 2–8.

55. Ibid., 105.

56. Levering, *Participatory Biblical Exegesis*, 18.

57. D. Stephen Long, *Speaking of God: Theology, Language, and Truth* (Grand Rapids, MI: Eerdmans, 2009), 86.

58. *Works*, 2:156–57.

59. Ibid., 158.

60. Scott J. Jones, *John Wesley's Conception and Use of Scripture* (Nashville: Abingdon, 1995), 48.

61. *The Works of John Wesley: Explanatory Notes on the New Testament*, ed. Thomas Jackson, repr. (Grand Rapids, MI: Zondervan, 1958–59); Rom. 12:6.

62. *Works*, 1:103. Here Outler's wording, "doctrine, rhetoric, and spirit" may correspond to Wesley's "intentions, affections, and practice."

63. *Works*, 1:106.

6. The Spread of Virtue and Happiness

1. Cited in *The Wesleyan Theological Heritage: Essays of Albert C. Outler*, ed. Thomas C. Oden and Leicester R. Longden (Grand Rapids, MI: Zondervan, 1991).

2. Outler, *The Wesleyan Theological Heritage*, 67–68.

3. Ibid.

4. *Works*, 1:222–23.

5. Ibid., 1:224.

6. Ibid., 1:208, 213–14.

7. Ibid., 1:408.

8. Ibid., 3:77.

9. Ibid., 3:97–98.

10. Christopher Thompson, *Christian Doctrine, Christian Identity: Augustine and the Narratives of Character* (Lanham, NY and Oxford: University Press of America, 1999), 99, cf. 78–91.

11. William H. Willimon, *Pastor: The Theology and Practice of Ordained Ministry* (Nashville: Abingdon, 2002), 199–200.

12. Robert L. Wilken, *The Spirit of Early Christian Thought: Seeking the Face of God* (New Haven, CT and London: Yale University Press, 2003), 262–72; Servais Pinckaers, O.P., *The Sources of Christian Ethics*, trans. Sr. Mary Thomas Noble, O.P. (Washington, DC: Catholic University Press of America, 1995), 1–44.

13. Wilken, *The Spirit of Early Christian Thought*, 275.

14. Saint Augustine, *The Lord's Sermon on the Mount*, trans. John J. Jepson, S.S., (New York and Mahway, NJ: Paulist, n.d.), 11–23, 125–27; see the commentary by Pinckaers in *The Sources of Christian Ethics*, 149–55.

15. Pinckaers, *The Sources of Christian Ethics*, 159–65.

16. Thomas Aquinas, *Summa Theologica*, trans. Fathers of the English Dominican Province, repr. (Allen, TX: Christian Classics, 1981), I–II. q108.3.

17. Simon Tugwell, *Albert and Thomas: Selected Writings* (New York: Paulist, 1988), 257.

18. Here I have followed the argument in Gilles Mongeau, S.J., "Aquinas's Spiritual Pedagogy," in *Nova et Vetera* 2:1 (Spring 2004): 91–114.

19. In this section I am following A. N. Williams, "Mystical Theology Redux: The Pattern of Aquinas' Summa Theologiae," in *Modern Theology* 13:1 (January 1997): 53–75. Hereafter references will be included in the body of the text.

20. Nicholas M. Healy, introduction to *Aquinas on Scripture: An Introduction to His Biblical Commentaries*, ed. Thomas Weinandy OFM, Daniel Keating, and John Yocum (London and New York: T&T Clark, 2004), 15–17; Henrik Rikhof, "Thomas on the Church: Reflections on a Sermon," in *Aquinas on Doctrine: A Critical Introduction*, ed. Thomas Weinandy, OFM, Daniel A. Keating, and John P. Yocum (London and New York: T&T Clark, 2004), 199–220.

21. Bruce Marshall, "*Quod Scit Una Uetula*: Aquinas on the Nature of Theology," in *The Theology of Thomas Aquinas*, ed. Rik Van Nieuwenhove and Joseph Wawrykow (Notre Dame, IN: University of Notre Dame Press, 2005), 14.

22. Pinckaers, *The Sources of Christian Ethics*, 221.

23. Nicholas M. Healy, *Thomas Aquinas: Theologian of the Christian Life* (Aldershot, UK and Burlington, VT: Ashgate, 2005), 135.

24. Fergus Kerr, O.P., *After Aquinas: Versions of Thomism* (London: Blackwell, 2002), 118.

25. Here I am following the discussion in A. N. Williams, *The Ground of Union: Deification in Aquinas and Palamas* (Oxford: Oxford University Press, 1999), and Jean-Pierre Torell, O.P., *Saint Thomas Aquinas: Spiritual Master*, trans. Robert Royal (Washington, DC: Catholic University of America Press, 2003), 2.82–88.

26. Nicholas Lash, *Believing Three Ways in One God* (Notre Dame, IN: University of Notre Dame Press, 1992), 20.

27. ST, Ia IIae qq. 1–5. See the good discussion in D. Juvenal Merriell, C.O., "Trinitarian Anthropology" in *The Theology of Thomas Aquinas*, ed. Rik Van Nieuwenhove and Joseph Wawrykow (Notre Dame, IN: University of Notre Dame Press, 2005).

28. Romanus Cessario, O.P., *The Virtues, Or the Examined Life* (New York and London: Continuum, 2002), 4–5.

29. Servais Pinckaers, O.P., *The Pinckaers Reader: Renewing Thomistic Moral Theology*, ed. John Berkman and Craig Steven Titus, trans. Sr. Mary Thomas Noble, O.P., Craig Steven Titus, Michael Sherwin, O.P., and Hugh Connolly (Washington, DC: Catholic University of America Press, 2005), 130–43.

30. Williams, *The Ground of Union*, 61–63.

31. See the excellent discussion in A. N. Williams, "Deification in the Summa Theologiae: A Structural Interpretation," *The Thomist* 61:2 (April 1997): 219–56.

32. Pinckaers, "Ethics and the Image of God," in *The Pinckaers Reader*, 132–40.

33. Healy, *Thomas Aquinas*, 111.

34. See the excellent discussion of the divine image in Romanus Cessario, O.P., *Christian Faith and the Theological Life* (Washington, DC: Catholic University of America Press, 1996), 38–48.

35. Williams, *The Ground of Union*, 55–64; Merriell, "Trinitarian Anthropology," 137–38.

36. Pinckaers, *The Sources of Theology*, 177–78.

37. ST, I.II. q. 69.

38. See Pinckaers's discussion of Aquinas and the Sermon on the Mount in "Beatitude and Beatitudes in the *Summa Theologiae*," *The Pinckaers Reader*, 115–29.

39. Matthew Levering, *Christ's Fulfillment of Torah and Temple: Salvation According to Thomas Aquinas* (Notre Dame, IN: University of Notre Dame Press, 2002), 145.

40. J. P. Torrell, O.P., *Saint Thomas Aquinas*, 2:166–67.

41. ST, I.II. qq. 27–28.

42. Fr. Cessario provides a good discussion of confession that is impelled by the presence of the Word and Spirit in *Christian Faith and the Theological Life*, 123–25.

43. See the thorough discussion in D. Stephen Long, *John Wesley's Moral Theology: The Quest of God and Goodness* (Nashville: Abingdon, 2005), chapter 5; although unavailable while this manuscript was being prepared, I strongly recommend Edgard A. Colon-Emeric, *Wesley, Aquinas, and Christian Perfection: An Ecumenical Dialogue* (Waco, TX: Baylor University Press, 2009).

44. *Works*, 1:481.

45. Long, *John Wesley's Moral Theology*, 130. See here the following: Richard B. Steele, *"Gracious Affection" and "True Virtue" According to Jonathan Edwards and John Wesley* (Metuchen, NJ: Scarecrow, 1994); Gregory Scott Clapper, *John Wesley on Religious Affections: His View on Experience and Emotion and Their Role in the Christian Life and Theology* (Metuchen, NJ: Scarecrow, 1989).

46. *Works*, 1:442.

47. Ibid., 443.

48. Long, *John Wesley's Moral Theology*, 140.

49. Cited by Outler in "An Introductory Comment," *Works*, 1:466.

50. *Works*, 1:470.

51. Ibid., 1:471–73.

52. Ibid., 1:473.

53. Ibid., 1:474–75; see the discussion of the Sermon on the Mount from the perspective of ethos, logos, and pathos in the work of Augustine, Chrysostom, and Luther by Jaroslav Pelikan, *Divine Rhetoric: The Sermon on the Mount as Message and Model in Augustine, Chrysostom, and Luther* (Crestwood, NY: St. Vladimir's Seminary Press, 2001), 97–150.

54. *Works*, 1:517.

55. Long, *John Wesley's Moral Theology*, 153–54.

56. *Works*, 1:518–20.

57. Ibid., 1:520, 529.

58. Ibid., 1:530.

59. Ibid., 1:107.

7. Preaching Theologians

1. Andrew Moore, *Realism and Christian Faith: God, Grammar, and Meaning* (Cambridge: Cambridge University Press, 2003), 118–19.

2. Ibid., 101–5; Daniel W. Hardy and David F. Ford, *Praising and Knowing God* (Philadelphia: Westminster, 1985), 6–23.

3. *Works*, 4:86–87.

4. Horton Davies, *Worship and Theology in England: Vol. III, From Watts and Wesley to Maurice, 1690–1850; Vol. IV, From Newman to Martineau, 1850–1900*, repr. (Grand Rapids, MI: Eerdmans, 1996), 3:143–209.

5. Randy L. Maddox, *Responsible Grace: John Wesley's Practical Theology* (Nashville: Kingswood Books, 1985), 113.

6. Nicholas M. Healy, *Thomas Aquinas: Theologian of the Christian Life* (Aldershot, UK and Burlington, VT: Ashgate, 2003), 21.

7. *Works*, 3:99.

8. William Abraham, "The End of Wesleyan Theology," *The Wesleyan Theological Journal* 40 (Spring): 22.

9. Martin Schmidt, "Wesley's Place in Church History," in *The Place of Wesley in the Christian Tradition: Essays Delivered in Celebration of the Commencement of the Publication of the Oxford Edition of the Works of John Wesley*, ed. Kenneth E. Rowe (Metuchen, NJ: Scarecrow, 1976), 71.

10. David F. Ford, *Christian Wisdom: Desiring God and Learning in Love* (Cambridge: Cambridge University Press, 2007), 225.

11. Albert Outler, *The Wesleyan Theological Heritage: Essays of Albert C. Outler*, ed. Thomas C. Oden and Leicester R. Longden (Grand Rapids, MI: Zondervan, 1991), 190.

12. Servais Pinckaers, O.P., *The Sources of Christian Ethics*, trans. Sr. Mary Thomas Nobel, O.P. (Washington, DC: Catholic University Press, 1995), 11.

13. *Works*, 1:452–53.

14. Ibid., 4:174–75.

15. Ibid., 4:174.

16. Ibid., 4:171–72.

17. See Outler's extensive introductory comments on Wesley's formulations of holiness in *John Wesley* (New York: Oxford University Press, 1964), 31.

18. *Works*, 4:144.

19. Abraham, "The End of Wesleyan Theology," 17-8.

20. Long, *John Wesley's Moral Theology*, 3-4.

21. *Works*, 4:69.

22. Ibid., 1:442.

23. Ibid., 3:189.

24. Ibid., xi, xiii.

25. Introduction to *Works*, 1:14–15.

26. Mark McIntosh, "Faith, Reason, and the Mind of Christ," in *Reason and the Reasons of Faith*, ed. Paul J. Griffiths and Reinhard Hutter (New York and London: T&T Clark, 2005), 139.

27. Simon Tugwell, O.P., *The Way of the Preacher* (Springfield, IL: Templegate, 1979), 31.

28. Geoffrey Wainwright, *Methodists in Dialog* (Nashville: Abingdon, 1995), 99.

29. McIntosh, "Faith, Reason, and the Mind of Christ," 137. I am indebted to McIntosh's discussion of the "mind of Christ."

30. *Works*, 3:586.